Great
Southern
Baptist
Evangelistic
Preaching

Great
Southern
Baptist
Evangelistic
Preaching

Edited by GERALD MARTIN
Foreword by Robert G. Lee

■

ZONDERVAN
PUBLISHING HOUSE
Grand Rapids, Michigan

*Dedicated to those laymen
who have contributed immeasurably to
my life and ministry.   Philippians 1:3*

FOREWORD

This book is appropriately named.

After reading the sermons—"The Marvel of Saving Grace," "The New Birth," "The Guttermost to the Uttermost," "The Real Evidence — Obedience," "The Saving of the Saved," "The Preservation of the Saints," "The Lost Are to Be Evangelized," "The Command to Be Filled With the Holy Spirit" — I evaluate all the sermons as great sermons as to content and phraseology. And, knowing as I do, the preachers of these sermons, I pronounce them great men of God — great by lip and life.

Strong adjectives of praise and appreciation can appropriately be used with reference to the sermons and the preachers of the sermons.

This book will enrich the lives of all who read — and will be a valuable addition to any library.

All preachers who read and study these sermons will be inspired and encouraged to be more proficient and Spirit-directed in their pulpit utterances.

In all these sermons, Jesus is exalted and the Bible honored. Superlatively worthwhile is this book — for every preacher, every Bible student, every church library, and every one who enjoys excellent preaching in the Word — with many practical applications of valuable truths.

ROBERT G. LEE

PREFACE

Southern Baptists have been known for their great evangelistic preaching. Their preachers have taken the Apostle as divinely inspired when he said, "Do the work of an evangelist." We have in our fold, scores of men who are capable full-time evangelists. God has given to most Southern Baptist pastors, the gift of evangelistic preaching. From the pulpits of our churches are heard the evangelistic appeals which were born in the heart of God and proclaimed by holy men of old.

This volume is merely "a taste" of evangelistic preaching which can be heard literally around the world in Southern Baptist pulpits.

From the first sermon to the last in this volume, these are examples of effectiveness. Dr. J. D. Grey, man of multiple talents has been a foremost preacher of evangelistic appeals in the city of New Orleans, Louisiana. All have seen the results which have come: a strong New Testament Church in a city which needs "a hot hearted" pulpit ministry and zealous witnessing ministry. Also the city, as a whole, has been lifted to a higher moral and spiritual plane by the results of this evangelistic preaching.

Turn to the last sermon in this volume and sample the ministry of Dr. W. A. Criswell. Many thought First Baptist Church, Dallas, Texas, had reached her peak before this man arrived on the scene. He has given himself primarily to a pulpit ministry and his ministry has been without ceasing, evangelistic. The results are seen in the growth of this great church in a time when men were saying the ministry of the downtown church had passed.

The day in which we are living raises a question as to the

effectiveness of evangelistic preaching. It is my own conviction that it is needed more in our day, when numerical results are smaller, than in earlier days when large numbers of people made public decisions for Christ.

May God continue to bless the world with evangelistic preachers and great evangelistic preaching.

CONTENTS

FOREWORD . . . . *Robert G. Lee*

PREFACE

1. THE MARVEL OF SAVING GRACE 13
J. D. Grey

2. THE NEW BIRTH 19
F. Stanley Hardee

3. THE GUTTERMOST TO THE UTTERMOST 29
Hugh R. Bumpas

4. OBEDIENCE — THE REAL EVIDENCE 35
Sterling Price

5. THE SAVING OF THE SAVED 47
Jaroy Weber

6. THE PRESERVATION OF THE SAINTS 59
A. B. Van Arsdale

7. THE LOST ARE TO BE EVANGELIZED 75
Paul Brooks Leath

8. THE PERSONS INVOLVED IN EVANGELISM 83
William M. Jones

9. THE POWER FOR EVANGELISM 92
Emory L. Williams

10. THE COMMAND TO BE FILLED WITH THE HOLY
SPIRIT 100
W. A. Criswell

1. *J. D. Grey**

THE MARVEL OF SAVING GRACE

". . . Why have I found grace in thine eyes, that thou shouldest take knowledge of me, seeing I am a stranger?" (Ruth 2:10).

This significant question which was asked by little Ruth in the long ago is a question which every child of God might ask of the Heavenly Father today. It is true that we are taking the words somewhat out of their setting and making them say something which Ruth did not definitely express, but just the same, the words of this question might be used by everyone of us, for surely when we contemplate all that God has done for us through Christ Jesus, and, further, when we consider our own unworthiness, we are prone to turn our

*J. D. GREY has been pastor of the First Baptist Church of New Orleans, Louisiana, since 1937. He is a graduate of Union University, Jackson, Tennessee; and of Southwestern Baptist Theological Seminary, Fort Worth, Texas. He holds three honorary degrees: D.D. Union University; LL.D. Louisiana College; D.D. Baylor University. He served as President of the Louisiana Baptist Convention for two terms and was elected President of the Southern Baptist Convention for two consecutive terms in 1951 and 1952. He serves on many denominational and civic boards and committees and has traveled all over the world in evangelistic and related activities.

faces to God and ask that question. "Why, but why, have I found grace in thine eyes?" So we are justified in saying that this little widow, Ruth, gave words of expression to our deepest heartfelt cry as she uttered this question in the long ago.

Then, if we view the text with its setting, in another light, we find complete justification for asking this question in the manner in which we use it today. The Lord Jesus Christ who shows such great grace to you and me is a descendant of the ruler Boaz of whom Ruth asked the question. It, therefore, becomes apparent that the great act of kindness and of love which was shown by Boaz toward the little woman Ruth is but a type of and a forecasting of a great grace which Christ is to show to you and to me and to everyone who will accept it.

As we look again at this question, and as we relate it to our standing before God, we who are saved are made to marvel at God's saving grace. Let us come closer to the question — let us apply it to the matter of salvation and let us ask again and again, "Why have I found grace in thine eyes, that thou shouldest take knowledge of me, seeing I am a stranger?"

Viewed in this light, the question at once becomes

A Plea of Amazement

The world marvels at the various miracles which our Lord performed while upon the earth. By His miraculous power the blind were made to see, the deaf were made to hear, the lame were made to walk and the dead were made to live. But no miracle which Jesus ever performed upon earth was as great as the miracle of His saving grace. Every now and then we meet someone who says he does not believe the miracles that are recorded in the New Testament. He doubts that Jesus did make the blind to see, the deaf to hear, the lame to walk, and the dead to live. But beloved friends, the miracles which Jesus continues to perform in the world cannot be doubted by any reasonable and fair-minded person. And the miracles of which I speak are the miracles of transformed lives. These miracles that walk and breathe about us today cannot be disputed.

This question of our text is the one great *why* of all the ages. More vital is it than why were worlds made, more important than why do wars come, more wonderful than why does the sun shine. It is the one great question which we cannot fathom, which we cannot comprehend and which we cannot explain. No, no one is able to explain why we have found grace in God's eyes. But even though we cannot explain it, we can accept it and we do accept it. There need be no doubt here for we accept many other things which we cannot explain. No scientist has ever been able to satisfactorily explain the love of a mother for her child. No biologist has ever succeeded in dissecting a mother's body and analyzing her love. So great and so wonderful is mother's love that it defies analysis and explanation. But we accept it as being vital and genuine and we are moved by it just the same. We cannot explain why God has shown His grace to poor sinful man except that He loved the world — but we are not kept from accepting that love because we cannot understand it. The question in our text is indeed a plea of amazement.

It is a marvel of transformation. Luther Burbank, the great scientist, has thrilled the world by his biological genius. He took an insignificant and unsightly daisy and transformed it into a glorious and beautiful Shasta daisy. He took the hated and despised cactus and by his skill removed all the stickers from it and gave the cattle country a spineless cactus that could be eaten by the cattle. He took the tiny, unsightly Irish potato and transformed it into a beautiful Burbank potato that gave great and good values to the multitudes. But beloved, no miracle of transformation in the plant kingdom which Luther Burbank ever performed compares at all favorably with the marvels which God's saving grace has wrought in multitudes of lives. The ugly life of a sinner has been transformed into something big and blessed and beautiful by God's saving grace.

Then, too, this plea of amazement tells us of the mystery of His cleansing power. One day Queen Victoria visited a large papermill at Windsor. She marvelled as she saw them place the dirty, greasy, filthy rags into the machines. These rags, that had been gathered up from the alleys and byways of England, were cleaned and made into beautiful, shining snow-white paper. So impressed was the Queen that the manager of the plant watermarked some of the paper with her own image. Beloved, this is no miracle greater than the one which happens when God takes a filthy, dirty, sinful man or woman and by the alchemy of His cleansing grace changes them. When one views these matters and studies this plea of amazement, who is not constrained to start singing aloud: "Amazing grace! how sweet the sound, That saved a wretch like me! I once was lost, but now am found, Was blind, but now I see."

In the second place, the question which is asked in our text becomes also:

AN ACCEPTANCE OF BENEFICENCE

Grace which is mentioned in the question of our text is the greatest of all of God's benefactions. God opens the windows of heaven and showers many blessings upon us every day. But this blessing, the blessing of grace, is the best blessing of all.

The beneficence referred to is described as this: "That thou shouldst take knowledge of me" — and that expression means to do good for us, just as Boaz did good for Ruth. Ruth was a poor little beggar woman, gleaning in the harvest fields of the rich and powerful Boaz. Boaz instructed his reapers to leave an abundance of grain for Ruth. He provided also that she should drink from his private vessels when she became thirsty. That is exactly what God has done for us in salvation. He has given the bread of life for us to satisfy our spiritual hunger and He has provided the water of life to slake our spiritual thirst.

This beneficence which is described and comprehended in the word "grace" means simply "unmerited favor." What did the poor little Moabitess Ruth have that she might purchase blessings from Boaz? She had nothing at all but Boaz showed unmerited favor or grace toward her. So it is with us. We were poor; we were undone. We had nothing by which we might purchase salvation but God the Father through Christ the Son showed His grace, His unmerited favor toward us in giving us salvation.

One final look at the words of our text indicates to us that it is also:

The Cry of Confession

Yes, and it is a cry of confession by contrast. Let us emphasize certain words which Ruth spoke in that question. She said, "why have *I* found grace in *thine* eyes that *thou* shouldst take knowledge of *me?*" Yes, little Ruth was thinking of that contrast. She was thinking of how poor and needy she was but how very wealthy and how high above her Boaz was. In this question she confessed her unworthiness. So it is, beloved, with you and with me. God is so good, so holy and so pure, and you and I were so lowly, so wretched, and so sinful; yet, God saw fit to show His grace toward us.

Indeed, it is a confession of our lowliness and our utter uselessness. Yet, God, knowing all about us, loves us and saves us just the same. The marvel of all marvels for you and me through life is expressed in the words of that song which we sang in childhood: "Wonderful things in the Bible

I see, This is the dearest, that Jesus loves me — I am so glad that Jesus loves me, Jesus loves even me."

Joseph Parker, the great preacher, was once asked why Jesus ever chose Judas Iscariot and the great old man of God replied with tears in his eyes, "I never bothered about why Jesus chose Judas Iscariot, but one thing that I shall never cease to marvel about is why Jesus chose Joseph Parker."

This confession which the text reveals touches also our lack of relation to God. Again notice the words of the question, "seeing I am a stranger." This identical word is used by the apostle Paul in Ephesians 2:12 when he spoke of us before we were saved. He said we were "strangers from the covenants of promise, having no hope, and without God in the world." But we were not only strangers; we were also enemies of God. In spite of that fact, God loved us and desired that we should come to Him.

Yes, God loves the worst sinner in the world and He will forgive that sinner if such a one will ask for forgiveness. I once heard the story of a girl who had drifted away from home into a big city. One night she was arrested in a disorderly house. In the police court she was hard and cynical but when a kindly Christian gentleman asked her for permission to write to her father she reluctantly told him to write and immediately her father wired that he had forgiven her and would receive her back to the sheltering love of the home. So great was the love which the father manifested that it melted her hard heart and brought her to repentance. So is it with the love of God the Father. It reaches to the hardest heart today. He offers the worst sinner who lives complete forgiveness if that one will confess his sins and fall into the loving, forgiving arms of the Father who for Christ's sake will forgive every sin. He then will say, "T'was grace that taught my heart to fear and grace my fears relieved; how precious did that grace appear, the hour I first believed."

2. *F. Stanley Hardee**

THE NEW BIRTH

During the Napoleonic wars, the emperors of Russia and France met one night on a raft in the middle of a German river for a conference. That conference changed the map of Europe.

Seventeen centuries earlier, the King of Heaven and a troubled ecclesiastical leader met on a flat Syrian roof. While the stars shone brightly, a discussion ensued which was destined to change the life of the inquirer . . . and the whole map of mankind.

The chief item at that conference table was the way a man may find the way to peace presently, and permanently. These men were fellow-countrymen . . . were of the same religious profession . . . and were teachers. But, a great gulf

*F. STANLY HARDEE, JR. is assistant to the President of New Orleans Baptist Theological Seminary. He has served churches in South Carolina, North Carolina and Louisiana. He is a graduate of Furman University, Presbyterian College (Clinton, South Carolina), Southeastern Seminary (Wake Forest, North Carolina), and New Orleans Seminary. He served as a member of the general board of the Baptist State Convention of North Carolina (of which he was Vice President) and on many other denominational committees and boards.

separated them: one was a person of the Spirit, the other a person of the flesh.

Jesus told Nicodemus, in certain terms, that he could bridge that chasm in only one way . . . the Way Up . . . the New Birth.

The modern church needs to return to that conference table. Having largely abandoned the message of the New Birth, the church " . . . does not major on the one thing that will solve the problems of our world-changed men. Man's basic problem is spiritual, not social (or otherwise). Man needs a complete change." (Billy Graham in an article in *Christianity Today*).

The central theme of Christianity is a new life, resulting from a New Birth. The thing which conquered pagan Rome was a group of Christians whose hearts Christ had touched, whose speech was filled with good will, whose conduct evidenced self-control.

Dr. H. Leo Eddleman has stated that we are in danger of trying to produce great Christians without preaching this fundamental truth . . . and it cannot be done.

In contemporary times, Dr. William L. Bennett, the illustrious pastor of the First Baptist Church in Fort Smith, Arkansas, has set the importance of this message in proper focus by stating, "We live in a world of guided missiles, but of misguided men. What we need is men divinely guided, but we have them only when they are born again."

From the Scriptures, let us note some *Highlights* of the New Testament prescription for modern men, divinely guided men on the *Way Up!*

First, note that

A MIGHTY CHANGE IS NECESSARY

. . . to be on the *way up!*

Jesus Asserted the Need

At that conference table, the first statement our Lord presented to Nicodemus was "You are on the wrong track . . . your nature must be changed." It hit him like a bombshell!!!

This was no *may* be statement . . . it was a *must* be demand!

God makes limited use of the word "must" in the Bible. Having a nature of persuasion, God pleads for volunteers instead of drafting them. Here, however, He makes it clear . . . there is only one way to enter the Kingdom . . . one *must* be born again.

This is *the divine imperative.* No note of luxury is heard from heaven's Son; here is presented an absolute necessity, an inescapable essential.

Man's Nature Demands It

By nature man is an alien to God. It all began when Adam committed suicide in the Garden bringing spiritual murder on all men (Romans 5:12).

As a consequence, man is born into a world where he not only has the possibility of sinning, but also probability that he *will* sin.

So . . . man's need is a soul need . . . a need resulting from sin — sin, which is not correctly described as a misguided impulse or a stumble in the right direction or a psychological abnormality, but sin which emanates from the heart that is deceitful and desperately wicked (Jeremiah 17:9).

This is what was wrong with the man who jumped to his death from the ninth floor of a Chicago hotel. His death note told the story: "I am worth ten million dollars as man judges things. But I am so poor in spirit that I cannot live longer. Something is terribly wrong with life." His nature needed changing . . . he needed to get on the *way up!* But, he went all the way down.

You see, there is no way to "patch up" our old self and serve Christ. Our fallen nature is bent on sinning . . . selfishness . . . hell . . . and there is no way to get on the upward way except through the New Birth.

The early days of this century were filled with delusions of grandeur. "We ourselves were so sure that at long last a generation had arisen, keen and eager, to put this disorderly earth right . . . and fit to do it . . . we meant so well, we tried so hard, and look what we have made of it. We can only muddle into muddle. What is required is a new kind of man," so said Walter Lippman.

One evening, after John Wesley had preached several times in succession on this text, some Christians asked, "Why do you keep preaching to us from this one text, 'Ye must be born again'?" To which Mr. Wesley replied, "Because, gentlemen, ye *must* be born again."

Pastors, let's preach that a mighty change is necessary to be on the way *up!* And it is . . . and it is!

Another highlight of the way *up* is that

REMARKABLE EXPRESSIONS WHICH DESCRIBES THE WAY UP . . . BORN AGAIN

Calvary Provided It

At the conference table on the Syrian roof, Jesus looked into that hungry-hearted Jew's face and gave the remarkable expression describing the way *up* — "You must be born again" (John 3:3).

Following Adam's spiritual suicide, God did not forsake man. The Old Testament is the magnificent story of God continuously reaching out seeking to bring man back to Himself. His redemptive activities led all the way to Calvary (Hebrews 1:1-3; John 3:16). There on Mount Calvary God, in bloody garments, dressed, courted, loved, bled and died. And why did He do it? To make being "born again" a possibility.

Jesus told Nicodemus that this is the way it would be — He would be lifted on the cross in order that men may be lifted on to the upward way . . . cleansed from their sins . . . born again.

Christ lifted up and put to shame on Calvary — this crucifixion cross is the ladder by which Christians enter into the holiest and are at length landed in glory.

Christ Proclaimed It

The sermon Christ preached to Nicodemus is the one He would have us preach, "You must be born again."

This was not simply an outward reformation, or such outward conformity as a proselyte might yield to a new set of rules of life. Had that been the case, Jesus would have proclaimed nothing more than the heathen philosophers, Socrates, Plato, or Aristotle, or than Nicodemus might have heard from any Rabbi about the duties of a proselyte from heathenism to Judaism.

So, to the Pharisee, proud of his birth, as a son of Abraham, Jesus said, "You must be born again."

Christians Have Pondered It

Dr. J. C. Ryle stated, "The change which our Lord here declares needful to salvation is evidently no slight or superficial one. It is not merely reformation, or amendment, or moral change, or outward alteration of life. It is a thorough change of heart, will and character. It is a passing from death to life. It is the implanting in our dead hearts of a new principle from above. It is the calling into existence of a new creature, with a new nature, new habits of life, new tastes, new desires, new appetites, new judgments, new opinions, new hopes, and new fears. All this, and nothing less than this is implied, when our Lord declares that we all need a 'new birth'!"

B. B. Warfield pondered it in this manner: "Being born again is a radical and complete transformation wrought in the soul (Romans 12:2; Ephesians 4:23) by God the Holy

Spirit (Titus 3:5; Ephesians 4:24), by virtue of which we become 'new men' (Ephesians 4:24; Colossians 3:10), no longer conformed to this world (Romans 12:2; Ephesians 4:22; Colossians 3:9), but in knowledge and holiness of the truth created after the image of God (Ephesians 4:24; Colossians 3:10; Romans 12:2)."

D. E. Y. Mullins put it this way: "Regeneration is the change wrought by the Spirit of God, by the use of truth as a means, in which the moral disposition of the soul is renewed in the image of Christ."

Dr. Herschel H. Hobbs notes that the term "New Birth" translates the Greek word *palingensia,* from *palin,* again and *genesis,* birth. It appears only twice in the New Testament (Matthew 19:28; Titus 3:5). Both instances are rendered regeneration. This idea is clearly set forth in John 3. The words "born again," or "born from above" denote birth.

Theologically, Christians have called this regeneration. To some this sounds "aged out," but there is no way to realize life "here and now" as well as "there and then" until one has experienced it — call it what you will.

It is our *main business* to get people regenerated, born again, on the way *up.*

Before a person lives, he "must have the nature of the King, a new nature that is imparted only by the Holy Spirit. When a man yields himself utterly to Christ, the Holy Spirit puts sight into blindness, hearing into deafness, health into disease, life into death."

Dr. Billy Graham, in *Peace With God,* discussed the New Birth as ". . . the infusing of divine life into the human soul . . . the implantation or impartation of divine nature into the human soul."

A person may be ignorant of many things in religion, and yet be saved. But to be ignorant of the matter of the New Birth is to be on the broad way to destruction . . . and not on the upward way.

A DIVINE FORMULA, FOLLOWED,
PROVIDES IT . . . THE WAY UP

"So you want to know the way?" said Jesus to Nicodemus. "Then, be born again."

"But how?" answered Nicodemus.

The answer of Jesus here and elsewhere assures kinship with the King . . . a new life . . . a new inheritance . . . the way *up!*

The Way Up Is Down

The way of the New Birth is through the joint act of repentance and faith.

Repentance has been described as " . . . the launching pad where the soul is sent on its eternal orbit with God at the center of the arc. When our hearts are bowed as low as they can get, and we truly acknowledge and forsake our sins, then God takes over as the second stage of a rocket, He lifts us toward His Kingdom."

It is true that the way *up* is down . . . for the word repentance is the translation of two Greek words in the New Testament. The first of these describes this emotional element — *metamelomai* — expressing regret . . . it may be of a godly sort leading to genuine repentance . . . or it may be a regret which produces no moral change (II Corinthians 7:9, 10; Luke 18:23; Matthew 27:3). Genuine repentance leads one to his knees (Luke 9:23).

The Way Up Is the Other Way

That other word translated repentance is *metanoia.* This word means a change of the mind or thought.

But the change of mind expressed by this word is more than a mere intellectual change of view. It carried with it the idea of will (Luke 3:8; cf. Acts 2:38; Romans 2:4; Mark 1:4, 15).

That concept is like this: one is going in one direction.

His sorrow for sin, his humility before God, his regret, lead him to make a 180-degree turn — to go the other way.

The Way Up Is Laying Hold

This includes commitment . . . surrender.

Comparing His death to the brazen serpent experience of the Old Testament, Jesus said that He had to be lifted up in order that unsaved, lost, damned men may lay hold on Him (believe) . . . thus never perishing . . . but having everlasting life.

This is coming in the spirit of this hymn:

"Nothing in my hand I bring, Simply to thy Cross I cling."

There is life in laying hold. The formula is simple . . . and if followed . . . puts a man on the way up.

REVOLUTIONARY LIFE ATTENDS IT . . . THE WAY UP!

It Produces a New Man

The world's foremost evangelist (Billy Graham) was exactly right when he declared, "Man can come to Christ by faith and emerge a new man. This sounds incredible — even impossible — and yet it is precisely what the Bible teaches."

This is entirely the work of the Holy Spirit. When Christ comes into one's heart by the formula stated, a new person emerges.

When Augustine came to Christ, he was lustful and timid — and Christ changed him.

When Zacchaeus met Christ in Jericho, he was greedy, and covetous — and Christ changed him.

When John Bunyan came to Christ, he was profane, crass, and dishonest — and Christ changed him.

When John Newton came to Christ, he was cruel, practical, and earthy — and Christ changed him so that he could sing:

"How sweet the name of Jesus sounds in a believer's ear!

It soothes his sorrows, heals his wounds, And drives away his fear."

You see, man emerges in faith with something new added — new nature (II Corinthians 5:17).

This is why Dr. Mullins called it a radical change of the moral and spiritual disposition.

Man Emerges With a New Set of Principles

These principles are enumerated in First John. The man who is born of God —

. . . believes that Jesus is the Christ.

. . . does not commit sin.

. . . does righteousness.

. . . loves the brethren.

. . . overcomes the world.

. . . keeps himself from the wicked one.

That is a man who has been born again, born of the Spirit. Where these principles are in evidence, there is a person who is on the way up — a man who has experienced the new birth — he is a child of the King.

Brothers, called of God, this New Birth is not a process — it is an "encounter experience."

It is my personal conviction that Nicodemus had such an experience. Expositors often abuse Nicodemus in their comments . . . they say he was a coward. It is well to remember that he and Joseph of Arimathea were so-called secret disciples; but when all the loud, shouting crowd ran away, those were the two who buried Jesus. "Sometimes," notes Dr. G. Campbell Morgan "there is more courage in quietness than in noise!"

Let us linger, however, let us not be fearful to speak. Rather . . . may the comment of Cyprian, Bishop of Carthage, to Donatus, be our testimony: " . . . They (the Christians) are masters of their souls . . . they have overcome the world . . . These people, Donatus, are Christians . . . and I am one of these."

Yes . . . say it . . . because it's *so* . . . say it and be glad . . . say it to share it, "Neighbor, I'm a Christian . . . I am one of these . . . I'm on the Way Up! And I want you to join me!"

> A ruler once came to Jesus by night
> To ask Him the way of salvation and light;
> The Master made answer in words true and plain,
> "Ye must be born again."

THIS IS THE WAY UP!

3. *Hugh R. Bumpas**

FROM THE GUTTERMOST
TO THE UTTERMOST

No wonder the Apostle Paul wrote to the people in that metropolis of the world, Rome, " . . . I am not ashamed of the gospel of Christ: for it is the power of God unto salvation to every one that believeth. . . " (Romans 1:16).

Dr. Ramsay Moore is a noted pediatrician who was elected one year as the head of the Pediatricians of Texas, and has practiced pediatrics and taught in the medical school in Dallas for many years. While thumbing through his well-marked Bible one day I noticed in the margin, next to the verse Romans 1:16, these words in red pencil mark: "Neither am I ashamed of the Gospel, Paul, signed, Dr. Ramsay Moore."

*HUGH R. BUMPAS is pastor of the Capitol Hill Baptist Church, Oklahoma City, Oklahoma. He is a graduate of Baylor University, Southwestern Baptist Theological Seminary (Th. M.) and Jackson College, Honolulu, Hawaii (D.D.), and has pastored several churches in Texas as well as participating in preaching missions to Alaska, Japan, Taiwan, Panama, Jamaica, Europe and the Holy Lands. He has been a member of the Southern Baptist Convention Executive Committee, the Southern Baptist Foundation, a past president of Baptist General Convention of Oklahoma, past vice president of the Home Mission Board, Southern Baptist Convention, and past president of the Southwestern Baptist Theological Seminary alumni.

Dr. Moore, nor the Apostle Paul, nor anyone else need ever be ashamed of the Gospel of Christ, because it is the power of God unto salvation, and to save from the guttermost to the uttermost.

He Is Able to Save From the Penalty of Sin, the Guilt

He said to the woman in Luke 7:50, " . . . Thy faith hath saved thee; go in peace." Paul says, "In whom we have redemption through his blood, even the forgiveness of sins" (Colossians 1:14).

The Associated Press carried an article a number of years ago about a woman named Mrs. Rose McMullen, whose blood had properly counteracted for the Staphylococcus Aures. The article told how she gave a transfusion and saved the life of a woman in Salt Lake City, and was flown immediately to New York to save the life of a young mother there. We cannot vouch for this story, but we can vouch for the story, the true story, that the Blood of Jesus Christ cleanses us from all sin.

He saves us from the power of sin. Paul says in Romans 6:17: "Know ye not, that to whom ye yield yourselves servants to obey, his servants ye are to whom ye obey; whether of sin unto death, or of obedience unto righteousness?" The writer of Hebrews says that Jesus was tempted in all points like as we (Hebrews 4:14-16). And yet, He overcame sin and gives us that victory.

He saves us from the presence of sin. I John 3:2 tells us that we may not look like full-fledged Christians now, but God is not through with us; and finally He will complete the job and take us from the presence of sin as well as from the penalty and from the power. Jude 24 promises us that He is not only able to save us, but to keep us from falling, and to carry us all the way through from the presence of sin. Those are tremendous words that Paul gives us in the eighth chapter of Romans, from the twenty-eighth verse to the end.

The writer in Hebrews says: "he is able to save us to the uttermost. . ." (Hebrews 8:25). The Scripture says: ". . . The just shall live by faith" (Romans 1:17). Salvation begins and centers and ends in Christ. And should I die at midnight tonight, and face God, I would say what they were singing in the song the night I was saved in the old Highland Baptist Church in Dallas, Texas, "Just as I am without one plea, but that Thy Blood was shed for me, and that Thou bid'st me come to Thee, O Lamb of God I come."

We can well say in the words of the song, "Nothing in my hands I bring, simply to Thy Cross I cling." Paul in II Timothy 1:12 said: "I know whom . . ." It was not a theory or a creed or system of religion, but it was a person on whom he depended. It is not Jesus or baptism. Not Jesus or the church. Nor Jesus or good works. Neither is it Jesus and baptism. Nor Jesus and the church. Nor Jesus and good works, but it is Jesus, and, Jesus alone, who does the full, complete, eternal job of saving us.

"HE IS ABLE TO SAVE TO THE UTTERMOST BECAUSE HE EVER LIVES TO MAKE AN ACCESSION."

He ever lives. We have visited the tombs of the founders of a number of religions, and the guide reminded us that here rested the body of the founder of that religion. But it was our privilege to walk inside and out again from the empty tomb of Jesus, and to realize the words of the song are true, "Up from the grave He arose, with a mighty triumph o'er His foes, He arose, He arose, Hallelujah! Christ arose."

We have a living and resurrected and ascended Saviour. And He ever lives to make intercession for us. Back in the Old Testament the high priest had one stone on each shoulder, representing all the tribes, and hence all the people of Israel (Exodus 22). He also had wore twelve stones on the breastplate over his heart, and when he went in to pray, it symbolized his bearing the people up in his strength, symbolized by his shoulders, and in his affections, symbolized by being over his heart. And so, Jesus, our high priest, intercedes for us, and the Bible says that He neither slumbers nor sleeps. And He carries us in His strength and in His affections, continually, before God.

It was a great thing to see Moses interceding for Israel, when God, because of their continued unfaithfulness, said He considered blotting them out. And Moses interceding in prayer said, "If you can't spare them, don't spare me either." I have a praying mother, for which I am thankful. But best of all intercessors is Jesus. Even after Peter lied and cursed at Jesus' trial, Jesus arose from the grave and He sent a special invitation, through the women, and said: "Go tell my disciples that I have risen — and Peter."

I can see Him extending that soon-to-be, nail-scarred hand to Peter and saying: "Peter, Satan has desired you that he might sift you as wheat, but I have prayed for you that your faith fail not" (paraphrase of Luke 16:31). And many a time I have been tempted and stumbled, but He always extended that great blood-stained, nail-scarred hand, and said: "Hugh, the devil has desired you that he might sift you as wheat, but I have prayed for you that your faith fail not." He is the offering and the priest. He is our advocate, and our propitiation for sins. I John 2:1 tells us that we have an advocate with the Father.

He Is Able to Save, Not Only to the Uttermost, But From the Guttermost.

On the banks of the shining Arno in Florence, Italy, is Michelangelo's piece of sculpture, David in all of his beauty and glory today. But this brilliant sculpture was chiseled from a piece of marble half buried in a junk heap in a back yard. And so Christ found us in degradation and sin, and lifted us and forgave us . . . saving us from the penalty and from the power, and finally, from the presence of sin.

Whom is He able to save so completely and to the uttermost? Everyone who comes to Him. Not he that joins the church, nor is baptized, nor performs good works, but he that comes to God, through Him. In John 14:6 Jesus said: "I am the way." He did not say that He was one of the ways, or the best way, or part of the way, or most of the way, but He said, "I am the way."

And it is so simple. We do not have to stand on our heads a half day at a time, or do great works, but simply come. I walk down the street and pass a neon sign that says: I.O.O.F. I am sure they are fine men, but I don't happen to be a member and I don't feel welcome in their secret meetings. And another sign says: Free Masons. They are fine men, but I don't happen to be a member and do not feel welcome in their secret meetings.

But I come to a great neon sign that says: "Whosoever will let him come." That includes me. As peculiar as my name is in this country, I found that in one of the Carolinas and in Tennessee, and again near Greenville, Texas, there are other men named Hugh Bumpas. And if God had put the name Hugh Bumpas in the Bible, I might have excused my being included, by saying, "That is one of the other men named Hugh Bumpas. But when He closed the last chapter of the last book of the Bible He said: "Whosoever will." That includes all the Hugh Bumpases. That includes me.

Years ago there was a man in our city who was manager of a taxicab company, who had given twenty-two years to drinking and gambling and cursing and most of the sins in the catalog. And one day he heard this Gospel and called us to his home, from the church where he had heard it, and Mr. Leland Mayberry, manager of the Capitol Hill Taxicab Company of Oklahoma City came to God, through this

Christ, at this invitation, and was saved from the guttermost to the uttermost.

The man who had been for twenty-two years a drunkard, a gambler, a cursing man, a man of all types of sin and iniquity, for these eight years has been a consistent, faithful, conscientious, praying, tithing, soul-winning, clean-living Christian, a faithful husband, a worthy father, and a valuable citizen of Oklahoma City.

He is a deacon, a Sunday school teacher, Chairman of the Soul-Winning Committee, helps to prepare the pastor and the candidates for baptism every Sunday night. He is at prayer meeting, Sunday school, morning and evening worship services, Training Union, goes out to visit weekly, and has led a number of his employees and others to Jesus Christ in these eight years. He is a living, walking example of this text that Jesus Christ is able to save from the guttermost to the uttermost. Trust Him as did Mr. Leland Mayberry, and the millions of others, and find that He is able, in your case, to save "from the guttermost to the uttermost."

4. *Sterling Price**

OBEDIENCE — THE REAL EVIDENCE

"And Samuel said, Hath the Lord as great delight in burnt offerings and sacrifices, as in obeying the voice of the Lord? Behold, to obey is better than sacrifice, and to hearken than the fat of rams" (I Samuel 15:22).

I want to think with you of Christ's conception of Christian obedience; what Jesus Christ expects His people to be both in their relationship toward Himself and toward the world.

We need in these days to recover the true relationship which should exist between our seeing and being, between our reception of His gifts and reflection of His character.

For in such a correlation of vision and life there is an

*DR. STERLING PRICE is pastor of the Third Baptist Church in St. Louis, Missouri. He has pastored there since January 1, 1959. Previous pastorates include: Calvary Baptist Church, Newport News, Virginia; First Baptist Church, Athens, Tennessee; and University Baptist Church, Abilene, Texas.

Dr. Price, a native of Oklahoma, is a graduate of Oklahoma Baptist University, Shawnee, Oklahoma and of Southwestern Baptist Theological Seminary, Fort Worth, Texas.

He has held such offices as President of the Southern Baptist Pastors' Conference, 1956; member of the Southern Baptist Executive Committee, 1960-66.

apologetic value which cannot be overstated, because I am persuaded that the discrepant lives of God's people are the main cause of a discredited Christ.

It is not the successful attack of blatant unbelievers, the daring denial of His existence which discredits Jesus Christ before the world, but rather the inconsistent lives of His people, the obvious difference between what we believe and what we are, between what we profess and what we manifest.

Here is to be seen the cause of much of the modern discredit cast upon the Name and Claim of Jesus Christ.

For, rightly or wrongly, the world takes its impression of Him from the manifestation and setting forth of His power in our lives.

Therefore our Christian profession is a matter of solemn and serious responsibility. It is not optional that I go in for holiness and the highest possible sanctity of life.

It is incumbent upon me as I name the name of Christ, so to represent Him before the world as that all who behold me may get a right conception of His grace and power and love.

This is the world's call, its justified demand. It is challenging our churches continually. "Invest your faith with visibility," they cry. "Show us your faith by your works."

I do not think the world cares much about our creeds or our doctrines; but when by grace we translate doctrines into deeds and creeds into character thus showing forth what Christ can be and do in human lives, then the world is convinced and attracted.

It is much easier to argue and defend one's theology, than it is to so live before men that others will see Jesus in you.

It is not enough to know the Scripture, we must live it. It is not enough to know Him who died that we might live, we must obediently follow Him, as ministers of the Word preaching the unsearchable riches of Christ to lost and dying men, as Christian business men and women in fair and honest dealings with our fellowmen.

I remember seeing once in a show window a display of seeds and bulbs, and passing them by with a mere glance. In the next window, however, there was a practical manifestation of the possibilities of those same seeds and bulbs in a showing of beautiful hyacinths and tulips.

These attracted me at once. The seeds had no power to attract my attention, to draw out my desire; but when I saw what they could produce then I understood their value and desired their beauty.

It is just so with our lives. The world cares but little about our preaching of the doctrines and principles of the Kingdom of God; but develop these living seeds, let men see the flowers and the fruit, let them become acquainted with their fragrance and lusciousness, and there is little doubt but that they will seek personal possession of the seed from which these have been produced.

A holy life is a supreme and surprising power to create in men the desire for Christ. Yes, obedience is the real evidence.

With these words of introduction, let me turn you to the words of Jesus in the fifteenth chapter of John, the fourteenth and fifteenth verses, in which is His plea for the evidence of Christian obedience:

"Ye are my friends, if ye do whatsoever I command you. Henceforth I call you not servants; for the servant knoweth not what his Lord doeth: but I have called you friends; for all things that I have heard of my Father I have made known unto you" (John 15:14, 15).

"YE ARE MY FRIENDS" (John 15:14a).

And if we get this conception firmly fixed in our minds so that it becomes the power and impulse of our lives, it will sanctify everything we do.

Like the vainly sought philosophers' stone of old, it will transform our common things into the gold of the glory of God, and will make all life shine with the radiance which cannot but attract beholders to Him who is its Author and its Power.

If we accept it afresh as an ideal of life that Christ wants us to live before the world as His friends, how wonderfully will our lives be transfigured!

"Ye are my friends" (John 15:14a): that is tantamount to saying that life is fellowship.

The lessons which we learned at the feet of Jesus are not merely intended to turn out good scholars but powerful men and women of faith and character whose service under the Lord Jesus Christ shall be obediently effective.

The story is told of an old Indian chief who, in gratitude for his new-found faith and joy, came to the missionary bearing in his hands a pair of beaded moccasins.

"Me give these to Jesus," he said, proffering them to the missionary.

But the missionary, looking at them shook his head and said, "No, chief, that is not what Jesus wants."

Bewildered, the old chief took them back to his tepee and this time brought some finely woven snowshoes. "No," said the missionary, "that is not what Jesus wants."

Finally, he went and secured from the wall of his tepee his most precious treasure . . . a well-oiled automatic rifle for which he had saved for years.

This he placed in the hands of the missionary, thinking it surely would be accepted; but the missionary handed back the rifle and said, "No, chief, that is not what Jesus wants."

The old chief stood there bewildered and in abject perplexity, not knowing what to do next. Then, as though a light had dawned, he lifted his eyes to the missionary and said, "Well, then, me give Jesus poor Indian, too."

The missionary replied, "That is it, chief. It is you yourself He wants, and nothing less will do."

You and I may bring to Christ the finely beaded moccasins of our service and run errands for Him; we may bring the snowshoes of our possessions; we may bring to Him, in utmost faith and belief, the finely polished rifle of the intellect; but until we say, "Lord, take poor Indian, too," and lay our hearts in His hand, the surrender never suffices.

This is the test of Friendship with our Blessed Lord.

"Ye Are The Light Of The World" (Matthew 5:14a)

I want to go further in this simple message by bringing to you another statement of Christ's as He seeks for our obedience, which is the real evidence, when He said to His disciples: "Ye are the light of the world" (Matthew 5:14a).

This is an emphasis upon the truth that no man lives unto himself. In making clear to His disciples the kind of life He intended them to live by the power of His grace, Christ plainly declared their relationship to the outside world.

There is no uncertainty in His teaching that He expects His people to occupy and maintain a unique position with regard to the world that knows Him not.

"Ye are [to be] the light of the world" (Matthew 5:14a).

There is here expressed a startling conjunction of His disciples with Himself for you will recollect in the eighth chapter of John and the twelfth verse He said of Himself, " . . . I am the light of the world . . . " (John 8:12); and now He applies to His disciples the very title which is pre-eminently His own.

All that was in Jesus Christ to illumine the world and to reveal the Father to men is to be in us.

Obedience is the real evidence if we are to be the light of the world.

"Let your light . . . shine" (Matthew 5:16a); remove the hindrances!

What did you *do* today that only a Christian would do?
What did you *say* today that was Christ speaking through you?
What do the people *see* who on your pathway fall?
Do they see you alone, or Christ as your all in all?

The true Christian is not a person who thanks God that he is better than other men, but one who desires in all humility to be better than he is.

It is a very solemn and serious thought, is it not? that we go out day by day in the world, we are going either to help or hinder some soul for eternity; we are either going to make it easier for some soul to find the pathway of life, or are going to make it more difficult.

We are either going to make divine realities clearer before others, so that they can see what we have apprehended, or we are going to obscure their vision.

Obedience, beloved, is the real evidence. "Let your light . . . shine" (Matthew 5:16a).

FOUR THINGS

Four things in any land must dwell
  If it endures and prospers well:
One is manhood true and good;
  One is noble womanhood;
One is child-life, clean and bright,
  And one an altar kept alight.
  "Let your light . . . shine" (Matthew 5:16a).

WHOSO DRAWS NIGH TO GOD

Whoso draws nigh to God one step
  Through doubtings dim,
God will advance a mile in bringing
  Light to him.
Lord, give me not just words to say,
  Though I need right words, too;
But strength to live in such a way
  My life will make my words come true.

We are tempted to use God when we ought to be used by God.

The extent of some people's religion is that they know the name of the church they stay away from.

The danger today is not so much that the world will force you to conform but that you will want to conform.

It is not by accident that the symbol of Christianity is the cross rather than a featherbed.

"YE SHALL RECEIVE POWER" (Acts 1:8a).

In pressing home the fact that obedience is the real evidence, I want to offer you Christ's words regarding the power by which the ideal may be realized, and by which the actual may be transformed.

"But ye shall receive power, after that the Holy Ghost is come upon you" (Acts 1:8a).

Power is the great conscious need of every one of us. There is not one of us who has not been made conscious in some degree of personal failure, impotency, insufficiency, and shortcoming.

The Archbishop of Canterbury once said that the Christian world needed new ideals, but I cannot but dissent from him in my heart.

What the Christian world needs is not new ideals, for we cannot have any higher, fairer, nobler, worthier ideals than those which Jesus our Lord has set before us.

What the Christian world needs in its corporate life and in the individual lives of its members is power to realize those ideals; power to walk according to the plan and pattern of which our Saviour has left us in no possible doubt.

"Ye shall receive *power*" (Acts 1:8a). Listen to this word, not to my interpretation of it, but to the Saviour's reiteration of this old word which we have heard again and again and let us each and all stretch out our hands in faith and receive the gifts of our Risen and Ascended Lord.

"But ye shall receive power, after that the Holy Ghost is come upon you" (Acts 1:8a).

The teaching of the New Testament with regard to Christian obedience is that it is not merely the imposition of a new perception but the inter-position of a new power, and that it is the power of a Person, the third Person of the Blessed Trinity; that our lives are not to be merely imitations of Christ but rather a reproduction and reduplication of His character in this divine power.

Power is not an influence, not a blessing, not something of a transient character, but a living Person who comes in to abide in our hearts forever.

"And when the day of Pentecost was fully come, they were all with one accord in one place. And suddenly there came a sound from heaven as of a rushing mighty wind, and it filled all the house where they were sitting. And there appeared unto them cloven tongues like as of fire, and it sat upon each of them. And they were all filled with the Holy Ghost" (Acts 2:1-4a).

Now Pentecost and all that it stands for is not merely a truth to be believed but an experience to be shared and a life to be lived.

The essential in Pentecost is not the rushing mighty wind nor the cloven tongues, but rather it is the impartation of the fullness of divine life to those who are called by the divine Name.

Disobedience is held up in the Bible as the blackest vice of the human heart. Disobedience is anarchy in God's Kingdom.

It is an attempting either to ignore or stab God in the back. God cares not for the sacrifice and ritual when your heart is not in them.

The mouth may sing His praises, but the feet must walk

in His way. The holy fires of God never come down upon a partial sacrifice, but only upon the whole.

The Jews knew only of a dead sacrifice. To the Jewish mind, to sacrifice meant to die, and so Paul's words were strange in their ears as he taught living sacrifices.

We do not need another Pentecost any more than we need another Calvary. What we do need is personal power for the conquest of the world through Christian obedience.

The story is told of a man who was strolling by a lake one day. There he saw a man getting ready to drown a little dog. "What's the matter with the dog?" he asked.

The man replied, "Well, I'll tell you. When Gypsy was a pup, we all loved him. But when he began to grow up, he was always wandering away, and we were always losing him. Now you know, a pup that follows everybody isn't any good to anybody."

The stroller thought for a moment how much the pup had been as he had been. He, too, had a Master, but the pull of the crowd meant a great deal more sometimes than the Master.

He was as anxious to please the crowd at times as he was to please Christ. There were many occasions when he had not had the courage nor the desire to follow the marks of his Lord's wounded feet.

"May I have the dog?" he said.

"Certainly," replied the owner.

He tucked the dog under his arm and strolled away. Perhaps some of us might say with that pup under our arm, "Well, Gypsy, when you and I follow everybody, we are no good to anybody. From now on you and I shall have one Master each. I shall be yours, and Christ shall be mine."

I am sure that a good many of us ought to come to some such decision. We ought to decide finally and forever whom we follow, and pray for the power to obediently follow Him.

"Ye Shall Be Witnesses" (Acts 1:8b).

In bringing this message to a close we are reminded that when Christ left His disciples He put into their hands one weapon for certain conquests in the conflict . . . the weapon of witnessing and sent them forth with the responsibility resting upon them of bearing witness before men.

Those of you who have been in London will recall the crypt of St. Paul's Cathedral and the monuments erected to many of the great men who have helped to make the history of England.

Amongst them you will remember is a small slab erected to the memory of the architect of the cathedral, Sir Christopher Wren. It is just a plain slab, quite unworthy in itself of the master architect, but its inscription says, "If you wish to see his memorial, look around you." That mighty cathedral is his best memorial, and needs no words to help proclaim his skill.

And it seems to me that our Lord sends us out into the world to be His lasting memorials before men. The one controlling passion in Christ's life was to fulfill His mission as a witness and if we are called by the same Blessed Name, it means consecration unto and consecration in the work of witnessing which does not, I fear, always characterize our lives.

The Holy Spirit witnesses to the heart of the believer, and the obedient believer witnesses to the world as an answering echo. You may make what you call an opening, but God can make an opportunity.

A young man was climbing rapidly to fame as a physician and diagnostician. His future was unusually bright, and the rungs of the ladder to success and fame seemed spaced advantageously for his own feet. In the very midst of this climb to professional power, he felt the call come to his heart to go to a foreign land as a medical missionary. His heart rebelled for a time, but the Voice of God was insistent and he finally surrendered to it.

One day after going as a medical missionary he said to a visiting minister, "If you would like to see a major operation be at the hospital at one o'clock." The minister stood on the balcony overlooking the operating table. The pitiless sun, beating on the roof of the hospital, and the ether fumes combined to give him a sense of nausea and he went out of the room to refresh himself.

He returned and the doctor was still operating. This he did four or five times, until seven long hours had passed. The last time he entered the operating room he noticed that the doctor had completed his last operation for the day. As they retired from the room, the minister said to him, "Doctor, is every day like this?"

The doctor looked at him. Beads of perspiration stood out on his forehead; his eyes were glassy; his lips were almost purple with the strain, and his hands began to tremble with fatigue. The minister said to him, "Doctor, how much would you have gotten for this operation in America?"

He replied, "Perhaps three or four hundred dollars . . . it was a complicated one." "How much will you receive for this?" the minister asked.

Looking at the poor native woman who had been wheeled into the operating room with only a copper in her hand, asking that in Christ's name he give her life, the doctor looked back at his friend and with tears welling up in those fine eyes and with a choke in his voice, he said, "Well, sir, for this I will get nothing but her gratitude and my Master's smile. But that, sir, is worth more than all the plaudits and money the world can give."

The preacher went out of the hospital that day coming to the conclusion that we are inestimable fools ever to be disobedient to the will of Christ. We never truly find our lives until first we lose them. To give them away to Christ in obedience is to keep them forever.

To obediently submit to His bondage is to know perfect freedom. The path we fear to see is often the path which alone will bring us the greatest satisfaction and happiness.

Obedience

I said, "Let me walk in the fields."
  He said, "No, walk in the town."
I said, "There are no flowers there."
  He said, "No flowers, but a crown."

I said, "But the skies are black
  There is nothing but noise and din."
And He wept as He sent me back . . .
  "There is more," He said, "there is sin."

I said, "But the air is thick,
  And fogs are veiling the sun."
He answered, "Yet souls are sick,
  And souls in the dark undone."

I said, "I shall miss the light,
  And friends will miss me, they say."
He answered, "Choose tonight
  If I am to miss you, or they."

I pleaded for time to be given.
  He said, "Is it hard to decide?
It will not seem hard in heaven
  To have followed the steps of your Guide."

I cast one look at the fields,
  Then set my face to the town;
He said, "My child, do you yield?
  Will you leave the flowers for the crown?"

Then into His hand went mine;
  And into my heart came He;
And I walk in a light divine,
  The path I had feared to see. [1]

[1] *Obedience* by George McDonald; E. P. Dutton & Company, New York. Used by permission.

5. *Jaroy Weber**

THE SAVING OF THE SAVED

"And the things that thou hast heard of me among many witnesses, the same commit thou to faithful men, who shall be able to teach others also" (II Timothy 2:2).

We have majored on saving the lost but minored on saving the saved. We have been busy making believers but failed to make disciples. It has been reported that last year more Baptists became non-resident members than were added to all our church rolls. If this continues we face self-liquidation within a few years. The Greek word for salvation embodies

* JAROY WEBER holds a B.A. degree from Louisiana College, and a D.D. from Louisiana Baptist College.

For ten years he was pastor of North Orange Baptist Church where he baptized 1,534 members.

In 1949, Dr. Weber accepted the pastorate of First Baptist Church in West Monroe, Louisiana, where he served for ten years.

Dr. Weber was pastor of First Baptist Church, Beaumont, Texas, for five years where he baptized 700 converts and received 1700 by letter and statement.

On September 1, 1966, Dr. Weber accepted the call of Dauphin Way Baptist Church in Mobile, Alabama. He is evangelistic in spirit and nature, and is outstanding in revival meetings, area crusades and evangelism conferences, speaking in many different states every year.

the thought of action which occurred in the past and is complete, but is also a progressive action which will continue indefinitely. Every Christian has been saved, is being saved and will be saved. We must remain interested in the initial experience but likewise in the future experience of putting into living reality the whole duty of a believer.

A Baptist pastor tells the story of an experience on his grandmother's farm. Late one afternoon she sent him out to coop the eight old hens. As he ran them through the door he counted them, all eight. To his surprise, he had nine, ten and more. He discovered that a board was missing off the back of the coop and the hens were getting out as fast as he put them in. This symbolizes the activity of the average church in the enlistment of its new members. Of the seven and one-half million Baptists on the rolls of our churches, one-fourth are A.W.O.L. and not saved to the cause. Dr. Vance Havner quotes an old preacher who said, "Some have said that we need a million more in fifty-four but if they are like the ones we already have, we are sunk." Every time we have a new convert added to the church we ought to have a new tither, a new Sunday school member, Training Union member, Brotherhood or W.M.U. member and another attendant to all the services of the church. One of our leaders states that unless we enlist a new member within the first six weeks after he joins, he will probably never be enlisted.

The membership of our church could be analyzed under several classifications of which I mention two. There is the division of three kinds: the self-conscious who have no clothes, the self-sufficient who have plenty of money and do not need the church, the self-deceived who think they are too busy to become active members of the church. Another classification is a division of six kinds: First, the growing in grace member, who is faithful, dependable and loyal to the total program of the church. Daily he is becoming a stronger

Christian as he grows in grace. Second, the contemporary member who lives by the standards of his associates. He lives no lower and yet no higher than the crowd with whom he associates. He drifts with what is current and popular. Third, the difficult group which contains those who are flagrant sinners who seek to hide their true nature and conduct from the church. They attempt to work themselves into responsible positions of the church, not in order to serve but to sever the fellowship of the church. It is this group which causes most of our problems and its members are perpetually hindering the program of God. The fourth is the problem group. They are sinners and know it. They want to find a solution to their problem and find power to live a victorious life. The fifth group consists of the troubled. The economic, social and domestic problems of drunkenness, divorce and discouragement, plague them. The sixth group consists of the down-and-outs. They are the alcoholics, the ones in jail, and those generally turned out by society. It is the perennial task of the preacher to properly integrate these groups into one common brotherhood of a Christian community.

I read an article sometime ago in a pastor's church bulletin, which stated that nearly every modern businessman was supposed to have at least one ulcer. Several reasons were listed as being chiefly responsible — one was the labor problem, another was the keen competition, high overhead and several other things. When I read this article I could not help thinking how many ulcers the poor businessman would have if he worked under trying circumstances as a pastor does.

Suppose, Mr. Business Man, you were overseer of 1,100 workers, (about the membership of our church), suppose that only 50 per cent of them ever showed up for work at any one time, and, of the remaining 50 per cent only about half of them with any degree of regularity. And, suppose that only one out of every five of your workers showed up after lunch (our evening services), and every time one of them had a slight headache or company to visit them they "took off" that day. And every time it thundered or even a slight flash of lightning appeared in the sky, 75 per cent of your workers pulled the cover over their heads and never appeared for duty that day. Suppose your workers only worked "when they felt like it," and still you must be sweet and never fire one of them. To get them to work you beg them, plead with them, pat them on the head, pet them, tickle them under the chin, and use every means under the sun to try to get them to do the work. And, suppose you were in competition with a notorious rascal (the devil) who had no scruples and was far more clever than you were and used such attractive things as fishing rods, soft pillows, T.V. programs, ball games, parties, pleasure drives, and a thousand and one other things to hurt your business.

Suppose your firm was heavily obligated to meet certain financial responsibilities and you had to depend upon your people to "give as they felt led" to carry out the biggest business in the world. So you think you have ulcers, Mr. Business Man, you ought to be in the shoes of a pastor for a while! Under God, Southern Baptists will undertake to do something about this tragic loss of human power which could be used to the glory of God!

We Ought to Save Them:

It is the command of Jesus; "Teaching them to observe all things whatsoever I have commanded you. . . " (Matthew 28:20).

A person is not completely saved until he has learned to obey all the commands of Christ and the teachings of the New Testament. The Great Commission is both an injunction to witness and train, to reach and teach, to save and serve. Dr. E. D. Head said, "A person is not truly evangelized until he becomes an evangel." The fruit to be genuine must be reproductive.

The need of the individual prompts us to save him. The Bible likens a new Christian to a babe needing the attention of its parents. The church is often willing to rejoice in the birth but not in the responsibility of caring for growth. It appears that the acccusation of the world concerning us is too often true. They say that we are interested in winning them to add to the church roll and have a larger member-ship, to be able to make an impressive report at the associa-tional meeting, to secure more money for salaries and build-ings, or just to boost our ego. The real reason is because every soul outside of Jesus Christ is lost and going to hell and woe is me if I preach not the gospel to them.

The March, 1955, issue of *Look* Magazine carries an article by Jerome Nathanson in which he states that sixty-four million Americans do not go to church. Mr. Nathanson, a leader in the New York Society for Ethical Culture, de-fends their position by stating that, "Many stay away be-cause of denominational rivalries and bickering. Some dis-like formal, elaborate rituals. And some (though they do not know it) follow the example of the noblest man our land has produced, Abraham Lincoln, who, in a startling and little-known statement of his faith, declared that he had never united with any church because he found difficulty in giving his assent, without mental reservations to the long, complicated statements of Christian doctrine which char-acterized articles of belief and confessions of faith." [1]

This statement, even though there is no defense for his concept, reveals man's basic need of an experience of sal-vation and an outlet of expressive service through the New Testament Church. Modern times find us adopting the ele-ments of Christianity which caused the period of the Dark

[1] *Look* Magazine, March 22, 1955, page 41.

Ages. In keeping alive the initial experience and joy of salvation we must not permit expectancy to give way to complacency, or creeds to replace personal experience, nor human manipulation to take the place of Holy Spirit action.

To save them is the hope of the future. We must save them for the sheer joy of it. Nothing saps the strength of the church like defeat from Satan. If God gives us a precious soul we must make every effort to utilize its every possibility to the glory of God. Every American takes delight in winning, whether it be in business, sports or religion. There is a vibrant note in the life of a church which has the thrill of saving people. This spiritual experience overshadows any other earthly experience a Christian can have. To witness people being saved from sin, self, normalcy, complacency, to full service of dedication is a joy — it is a thrill!

We must save them for food. No other spiritual food will keep alive God's workers like winning victories against Satan and snatching souls and lives out of the sin of indifference. On the tidal wave of revival in the midst of God's people, sweeps in the answer to every church problem. This is the solution to fellowship, discipleship, stewardship, etc. No church can grow which continues to add names to its roll but not lives to its ranks.

We ought to save them for funds. Every missionary on the field of service will be called home, every orphanage, hospital, seminary and college will be closed, every church will have to tack up a sign on its front door, "For Sale," unless we save the additions and teach them to become good stewards of their possessions to continue the work of God. The church must save them so they can in turn save the church!

WE CAN SAVE THEM:

We have the helps. First, fellowship in a Baptist church is the most wholesome to be found anywhere. The spirit of democracy among the saints presents a liberty and participation second to none. We ought to continue making this fellowship so vibrant and exciting that our members will be more loyal and faithful to our services than many are to their clubs and fraternities.

The second help is our facilities. No more are we just a despised sect shoved off into some obscure area of the city in a dilapidated one-room building. Today our mighty church plants stand in the most prominent places in our cities. Millions of dollars have been invested in worship centers, educational departments, and recreational facilities as available instruments to save our people from going back into a life with the world. Today as never before the church ought to provide a seven-day-a-week program that will meet every phase of complex life — socially, mentally, physically and religiously.

Our hindrances are many. The caste system in American life, as expressed in social and financial differences, poses a problem of proper integration for new members. By preaching and practicing the equality of believers in Christ, we can overcome this feeling of unwelcome on the part of members.

A selfish, egocentric attitude on the part of members causes them to lack a personal interest in other people. This creates a feeling of intrusion in the minds of new converts if they are placed in this environment.

One of the chief hindrances is the fact that the church doesn't see the ultimate worth of the individual to the kingdom of God and thus ignores its opportunity to help in the development of new babes in Christ.

WE WILL SAVE THEM:

For a church to say, "This year we will major on saving and conserving souls," is rather facetious since evangelism is the primary task of the church. It would be like an oil refinery advertising that this year it would major in producing oil or a paper mill to decide to make paper. What other business does an oil refinery have, or a paper mill, or a church?

We must propose to do it. The first step is to make the reception into church membership a meaningful experience. Too often we take this lightly and leave the impression that the church is to be grateful to the person for uniting with her. The feeling of gratitude ought to be on the part of the new convert, for to have partnership with Christ and fellow Christians is the greatest enterprise in the world, to possess citizenship in the greatest kingdom known among men is life's greatest privilege. Many honors of high degree come to mortal man but none to compare with that of being a regenerated, consecrated, dedicated member of the divine-human institution which Christ founded and of which He is the living head. Along with this feeling of privilege ought to be created a sense of duty and obligation to the church. A church is due something from every member and when a person neglects this obligation it bespeaks a serious moral failure. Our high pressure methods of enlistment too often imply that converts will do the church honor with their membership rather than a commitment of life to the church of Jesus Christ.

Not only are we to make their reception into membership meaningful but the recognition must be one which gives the person a sense of friendly welcome. Too often as they come forward in a service to take the pastor's hand the result is a cold, mechanical motion and second to receive them. The pastor ought to give time and attention to this opportunity to personalize this experience by introducing these new members to the congregation by giving name, address, family ties, occupation and any information of special interest. This must not be cut and dried, a formal gesture, but one of genuine sincerity. Perhaps the way they used to do it in churches, by having the folks stand and give their conversion experiences, would emphasize the spiritual content of this occasion.

We must not only give them recognition but also responsibility. The legend, to use them or lose them, is still true. There are conflicting viewpoints relative to churches becoming too large. A church is never too large as long as its program includes a definite responsibility for every member and develops him in Christian growth. However, unless one is working for his or her religion by using the talents in service which the Lord gave to each, that person becomes discouraged or indifferent, and then moves on to another church to secure that spiritual happiness for which his or her heart yearns, or ceases to attend any church and begins a search for happiness in the world.

We must preach to do it. We, as pastors must not only purpose to save the saved but must preach to do it. Ours must be a type of preaching which will indoctrinate our members with the teachings of God's Word so that they may be strong in faith once delivered to the saints. This need not be a dead formalistic creedal presentation of old truth but a living dynamic warm-hearted presentation of truth. Too much of our present-day preaching is apologetic rather than authoritative. People are not interested in the theories of the atonement, the exegesis of Logos, the iota sub-script of New Testament writings, or Hammurabi's Code. They want to know how the teachings of Christ can apply to their life as they live in the modern twentieth century crisis.

R. A. Torrey's statement is worthy of consideration. Said he, "I preach four great truths. I preach the whole Bible from cover to cover. I preach the power of the blood of Jesus Christ to save — the doctrine of the Atonement. I preach the personality of the Holy Spirit. I preach the power of prayer." On March 12, 1955, George Sokolsky wrote an editorial column on, "Why is Billy Graham so popular?" He stated, "Because he talks religion. Too many clergymen, in their sermons these days, do not talk religion. They talk about everything else. They review books of temporary value; they review Broadway plays; they are amateur psychiatrists; they go in for social action; they turn the pulpit into a political forum. But they do not talk of man's relation to God and of the evil of sin and of the consequences of infractions of the moral law. Since they are not being God's messengers, their sermons become tiresome and are often trite, and the congregants find golf more amusing or give themselves a few hours to 'do it yourself' occupations at home."

A return to simple Biblical preaching is needed in every pulpit if we are to win our members. Whether our method of preaching is the oratorical style of Freulinghonsen, the Father of the Great Awakening, or the quiet, calm reader like Jonathan Edwards, we ought to preach a message from God to the hearts of the people. Taylor had it right when he said, "The business of the preacher is to take something hot out of his own heart and shove it into mine."

We must have a program to do it. The intent of my message is not to give the program, because the department of evangelism has provided such, but my purpose is to provide the motive and impetus for carrying it out. Every church can have the instruction class for new members, taught by the pastor on Sunday evening. To welcome the new members a supper can be given in their honor, at which time you introduce them to the leadership personnel of your church. At this supper, you assign them with another member who will be their "buddy" for a six-weeks period. The purpose of this is that the established member can aid the new member in acquainting himself with the program of the church and seek to enlist him in all the activities of the church. A constant report is made by the "buddies" to see if the new members are being assimilated properly. Along with this personalized effort the pastor can call on the new member during the week he unites with the church to discuss his spiritual decision and growth. The educational director can call on the member the same week to discuss the opportunities of service, including the stewardship responsibility, and seek to enlist him. Then, these names are given to the unit organization in which they would belong and are encouraged to enlist by every unit in the church. Once a year it is good to have a roll call service for the new members who joined during the previous year as a means of analyzing the results of your enlistment program.

Dr. Andrew W. Blackwood said, "A pastor's failure is not due to his lack of ability or charm but to his lack of a divine purpose." This encourages me to believe that any pastor or church can successively maintain a program to save the unenlisted majority. This will not be easy but since Baptists are known as hard workers, it can be accomplished. Likewise, we must make every possible effort to keep our church close to the people and applicable to everyday problems. Caution should be given against the danger of developing a class-structured membership which would appeal to the complacency of the middle class. Our strength lies in our emphasis on the Bible and its answer for every problem. From these great pillars of faith we must never depart.

When the saved are saved then we can join in singing with the poet:

From all the dark places of earth's heathen races
O see how the thick shadows fly!
The voice of salvation awakes every nation,
Come over and help us, they cry.
With shouting and singing and jubilant ringing,
Their arms of rebellion cast down;
At last every nation the Lord of salvation,

Their King and Redeemer shall crown!
The kingdom is coming, O tell ye the story,
God's banner exalted shall be!
The earth shall be full of His knowledge and glory,
As waters that cover the sea.

6. *A. B. Van Arsdale**

THE PRESERVATION OF THE SAINTS

Scripture: I John 5:10b-12.

Jesus said, "No man can serve two masters. . ." (Matthew 6:24). That statement is applicable to the Christian as well as to the non-Christian. Self or the Saviour must be the polestar around which all activity rotates. In the final analysis all religious activity is either ego-centric or Christo-centric. If one is religious in order to be saved, then the life is lived in slavish fear and in agonized activity purely for self; it is ego-centric. If one is religious because he has been saved, then all activity is for the sake of Christ; it is Christo-centric. One's view of the security of the believer will determine whether religious activity is self-centered or Christ-centered.

If one must hold out faithful to the end, if one must work out his own salvation with fear and trembling, then all religious activity is ultimately selfish. But if one is held faith-

*A. B. VAN ARSDALE is a graduate of Decatur Baptist College (Decatur, Texas), Baylor University (Waco, Texas), and Southwestern Seminary (Fort Worth, Texas). He has held pastorates in Texas and Arkansas, and is presently pastor of the Central Baptist Church of Decatur, Alabama. He has been active on committees and boards throughout his denomination, and is currently a trustee of Southwestern Seminary.

fully by Christ, if one works out what Christ has worked in, then all Christian activity is for the glory of the Christ. The purpose of this message is to show that the latter is the message of the Bible.

As a boy on a farm just a few miles from Louisiana, Ky., I learned that it is advisable to clear out the underbrush before applying the axe to the tree. Permit me to clear the underbrush by making some general observations before coming to the main message.

First, it is impossible to cover all the ground in one message, especially in one of twenty-five or thirty minutes. Some scriptures and arguments must be ignored and others can only be touched lightly.

Second, we must acknowledge that no human being can factually say whether another is a Christian or not for "man looketh on the outward appearance, but the Lord looketh on the heart" (I Samuel 16:7). This closes the door to the old argument, "I knew a person who was saved, then fell away." We can neither be certain he was saved nor that he isn't now.

Third, we must ever keep in mind the dual nature of man. Man is a spirit but he has a body. That experience known as the New Birth brings life to the spirit, but physically Paul says we are yet "waiting for the adoption, to wit, the redemption of our body" (Romans 8:23). Thank God the body will yet be glorified in the resurrection, but meanwhile the tug of the flesh frequently produces what the Bible speaks of as carnal Christians. They may be saved but the physical side gains the upper hand.

Fourth, this doctrine does not preclude the possibility of sin. It is not synonymous with sinless perfection. John, the great exponent of "eternal life," flatly states, "If we say that we have no sin [present tense], we deceive ourselves, and the truth is not in us" (I John 1:8). As a matter of fact, the more Christlike we are, the more aware of sin we are. The greater concept we have of God, the greater consciousness we have of sin. A Christian sins and he knows it. For this reason Jesus taught Christians to pray "forgive us our sins. . ." (Luke 11:4).

Fifth, this doctrine is not a license to sin. Repeatedly we hear, "If I believe such a doctrine, I would do as I want to do since I would be saved regardless." I like the answer of Dr. W. T. Conner, "That's right. I do what I want to do, but in regeneration Christ did something to my wanter. I just don't want to do the things you are talking about." Let us never forget that the New Birth creates a hatred in man's heart for sin, and he doesn't want to do that which is wrong.

Sixth, this truth is not to be sustained by mere opinion or human analogy. Frequently, the argument is presented that when a child is once born to its parents, it cannot become unborn. That statement is true. But a disinherited child would have little joy or profit in the relationship, and children are sometimes disinherited. Just so, should God disinherit one of His own, it is hard to conceive just what the relationship would be. The human analogy, when followed just so far, is fine; but when followed out logically, it breaks down. The preservation of the saints must depend upon more solid ground than this.

Seventh, we must depend upon a "thus saith the Lord." Thank God, there is much of this nature. God has spoken frequently concerning the security of His saints. I propose to pick out several great truths that form indestructible pillars supporting the security of the believer as the capstone. Man is not a spider to spin the web of his own salvation, but he does not need to be for his Saviour has promised to meet his every need.

Before considering God's preservation permit me to present the seemingly contradictory but really complementary subject of the —

PERSEVERANCE OF THE SAINTS

Multitudes of church members go into spiritual orbit and shout "hosanna" when the message is on Preservation, but then develop a chill and become mute when the subject is Perseverance. Yet none can deny that Jesus said "he that endureth to the end shall be saved" (Matthew 10:22), and repeated practically the same statement in Matthew 24:13. I am fully mindful that some scholars assign these scriptures exclusively to the Jews and especially during the Tribulation. Grant, for the sake of argument, that the application primarily is to that people at that time, yet the underlying truth is applicable to all of God's people of all times. Surely even the ultra-dispensationalist will agree the parable of the sower deals with our day. Therein our Lord spoke of the seed falling on stony ground and quickly withering after a promising start. In Matthew 13:20, 21 is His explanation. It pictures one joyously receiving the Gospel, yet, lacking depth, he "endureth for a while" but is offended when troubles come. His very lack of perseverance is used by Jesus to demonstrate a superficial response. Then He went on to tell of good seed falling on good ground and bringing forth fruit. It persevered until harvest. Similar is His teaching in the parable of the Vine and Branches. ". . . He that abideth in me, and I in him, the same bringeth forth much fruit. . ." (John 15:5), but added in verse 6 "If a man abide not in me, he is cast forth. . . ." This is not teaching what some call falling from grace. The lesson is simple. Unless the branch continues until fruit appears, it has not really contacted the life-giving substance of the vine; and unless a man perseveres until the fruit of godliness appears, he has never really contacted the God-life.

In like manner, James argues ". . . faith, if it hath not works, is dead. . ." and rightly declares ". . . shew me thy faith without thy works, and I will shew thee my faith by my works" (James 2:17, 18). He is simply stating there is no genuine saving faith unless it is manifested in persevering labor for Christ. Jesus affirmed the same truth in the words ". . . If a man love me, he will keep my words. . . " (John 14: 23). If one professes faith but doeth not His words, his hope is as foolish as one building a house on the sand. So said Jesus as He concluded His sermon on the mount.

Beloved, hear me! A truly redeemed sinner will labor to please his Master. He may sin and stumble, but will hate his sin and arise to try again. It is this persevering believer that God will preserve. Now, permit me to present the great undergirding truths:

The first one is the

PURPOSE OF GOD

I know of no great theologian who does not gladly admit that salvation begins with the divine purpose. The prophet Jonah declared ". . . Salvation is of the Lord" (Jonah 2:9). The Apostle Paul wrote of "them who are the called according to his purpose" (Romans 8:28). In the following two verses he outlines a five-fold divine activity in connection with the experience of salvation. God is depicted as having foreknown, predestinated, called, justified, and glorified the penitent believer in order that the latter might "be conformed to the image of His Son, that He might be the first born among many brethren." Every true child of God has already experienced the first four of these divine actions. Since Christ is "glorified," and God is timeless, the glorification of God's child is also listed as an accomplished fact being an aorist tense in the Greek. We need not completely comprehend this foreknowledge and predestinating work of God in order to profit by it any more than we need to thoroughly understand all about the wind in order to set a sail before it. Somehow, someway the purpose of God, based upon His foreknowledge, launches the gracious work of redemption in a man and is never complete short of glorification. He knows the end from the beginning, He is the Alpha and Omega. He never acts foolishly. He is never caught shorthanded. All of His acts are based upon absolute knowledge. When He launches the work of redemption in the life of an individual, He knows the ultimate outcome of His purposive grace.

Now think a moment! Paul used the word "justified" to cover the actual saving experience that comes to one who totally commits himself to Christ as Lord and Saviour. Paul clearly states that we are "justified by His blood. . ." (Romans 5:9). He tasted death for every man; His blood is sufficient for all. All men can be saved through His blood. But it is also true that for even one man to be saved Christ would have had to die upon the cross. And that man must have been included in the mystifying gracious purpose of God. Tell me! How can you reconcile the redemptive purpose of God, based upon absolute foreknowledge, saving a man for thirty days or thirty years yet knowing all the time the man would so sin as to lose it all? Remember Christ would have had to die on the cross for that man to be saved for even one hour had all the rest of mankind rejected Him. Would the all-wise God have purposed the salvation of that man while foreseeing the final result of failure? His purpose has failed unless that man is "glorified" even as Christ is now glorified. Say not so! "Whom he foreknew . . . he justified: and whom he justified, them he also glorified." Fundamentally, one's salvation depends upon the eternal purpose of a redeeming God and not on the erratic practices of sin-weakened man.

Our second great pillar is the
PROVIDENCE OF GOD

The God I worship is the Almighty. All of His Almightiness is cast into the battle to save His own. God gloried in the manifestation of His Almightiness in creation. But His greatest glory comes from the redemption of a sin-scarred, hell-bound sinner. When once that redemption comes to a sinner, God will never permit Satan to rob Him of His glory by snatching that Christian from Him. Paul states, ". . . we know that all things work together for good to them that love God. . ." (Romans 8:28). Here is the guarantee that every wheel in the providence of God revolves for the good of the Christian, whether it be "the world, or life, or death, or things present, or things to come; all are yours; And ye are Christ's; and Christ is God's" (I Corinthians 3:22, 23). Many things, standing alone, may appear harmful. But wait until the full story is told. The God who could make the evil designs of Joseph's brethren work for good, and cause the cunning Caiaphas to truthfully set forth redemption's story can certainly see that everything when put together, works for my good. If all works together for good, then nothing is left to destroy my salvation.

To the strong and mighty supporting pillars we can now add the

POSITION OF GOD'S CHILDREN

Two small phrases, found repeatedly in the New Testament, are fundamentally significant. ". . . if any man be in Christ. . ." (II Corinthians 5:17) and ". . . Christ in you, the hope of glory" (Colossians 1:27). Note them well, "in Christ" and "Christ in you"! Together they speak of the vital relationship of the Saviour and the saved and of the position of the redeemed. Paul proclaimed that faith unites the believer with Christ, that the believer is made one with Him. In Him we are justified, are made new creatures, and reconciled, are made children of God. So vital is that union and position of the Christian that Paul states that he no longer lives, but Christ lives in him (Galatians 2:20). And the great apostle states that there is no power that can destroy that relationship. Listen to him, "Who shall separate us from the love of Christ? shall tribulation, or distress, or persecution, or famine, or nakedness, or peril, or sword?," and then his triumphant shout, "Nay, in all these things we are more than conquerors through him that loved us" (Romans 8:35, 37). The union is as permanent as the power of God for it is maintained "through Him" and not through the vacillating efforts of man.

That picture, so often seen in stained glass windows of churches, is a libel on Christianity. It is a picture of a woman with long flowing hair clinging with numbed fingers to a cross-shaped rock rising from the storm. No, no, no! My salvation does not depend upon my clinging to a cold slippery rock. Thank God, I am *in* the "Rock of Ages, cleft for me."

Let me emphasize this vital matter. The Bible repeatedly teaches that nothing can destroy that position produced by our relationship with Christ. Satan cannot do it. John declares, ". . . the One who was begotten of God carefully watches over and protects him — Christ's divine presence within him preserves him against the evil — and the wicked one does not lay hold (get a grip) on him or touch [him]" (I John 5:18, *The Amplified Bible*). Notice it is Christ that keeps us. Prior to his trial by fire, Simon Peter boasted of his fidelity. Jesus then told him that Satan had asked for him (Luke 22:31, 32). Satan can do nothing to a Christian apart from God's permission. That same truth is graphically pictured in the experience of Job. And a loving Father will never permit the arch-enemy to destroy one of His children. Satan with all his diabolical power cannot wreck the believer's position "in Christ."

Sin can't do it "For sin shall not have dominion over you. . ." (Romans 6:14). Everyone who holds the idea of falling from grace must answer this question, "How much sin would be necessary for a Christian to be lost?" The

Bible simply says, "The soul that sinneth, it shall die" (Ezekiel 18:4). It doesn't say the soul that sinneth much, but the soul that sinneth. If any amount of sin could take a redeemed soul from God, then one sin could do it. Then no one could ever know whether he was saved or not for all of us sin scores of times daily. But the Bible says that sin shall not have dominion. All of a Christian's sins are under the blood. Sin on the part of a Christian does not dissolve the vital union.

Temptation can't do it for "God is faithful, who will not suffer you to be tempted above that ye are able; but will with the temptation also make a way to escape, that ye may be able to bear it" (I Corinthians 10:13).

The world can't do it for "this is the victory that overcometh the world, even our faith" (I John 5:4).

God says He won't do it but "him that cometh to me I will in no wise cast out" (John 6:37). Note these words, "in no wise." Nothing can cause Him to do it.

And John 3:16 suggests that man himself cannot do it. The word "perish" has as its root meaning "to destroy." It is a subjunctive mood, suggesting emphatic negation, and is a middle voice carrying the reflexive idea. Read it that way, "whosoever believeth in him, shall not in any wise destroy himself."

Paul concludes the whole matter in Romans 8:38, 39 by saying that nothing in existence, "life or death"; nothing among spiritual forces, "angels, principalities, nor powers"; nothing in time, "things present nor things to come"; and nothing in space, "nor height nor depth," could separate from the love of God. Then, lest he had overlooked something, he added, "nor any other created thing." The Christian is united with Christ, he is in Christ, and nothing here or hereafter can break that union.

Consider now the fourth pillar, the

PROPERTIES OF GOD'S CHILDREN

When Paul wrote, "If any man be in Christ, he is a new creature," he revealed an amazing truth. A Christian is a new man, not a revamped model. His newness includes an entirely different nature. Listen to Simon Peter, "Whereby are given unto us exceeding great and precious promises: that by these ye might be partakers of the divine nature. . ." (II Peter 1:4). In regeneration God's nature to some extent at least is imparted to the believing soul. That nature which enables man to escape the corruption of the world comes from an incorruptible seed, "Being born again not of corruptible seed, but of incorruptible, by the word of God, which liveth and abideth for ever" (I Peter 1:23). All over our world farmers spend millions of dollars looking for a perfect seed. They do so because of confidence in the law of the harvest that "whatsoever a man soweth, that shall he also reap." If they could find a perfect seed, they could expect a perfect harvest. In the spiritual realm that perfect seed has been provided and is available. It is the Word of God, incorruptible, that liveth and abideth forever. That perfect seed, bearing the nature of God, planted in man's heart produces a new creature in God's image, an incorruptible creature that liveth and abideth forever.

Of utmost importance in consideration of this new nature of the Christian is the statement of Jesus, ". . . I give unto them eternal life. . ." (John 10:28). John is peculiarly the apostle of eternal life. Repeatedly does he use the term. He picked out that promise of Jesus and reiterated it, "And this is the promise that he hath promised us, even eternal life" (I John 2:25). That is the only kind of life He ever promised. As the beloved apostle used the term, it is more qualitative than quantitative. It is more a description of the life than the duration that is in view. What kind of life is it

that Jesus gives? Is not the answer found in His own words
". . . I am the . . . life. . . ." (John 14:6)? Every student of
the Scripture knows that Jesus here identified Himself with
the great "I AM" of the Old Testament, the eternal self-exist-
ent God. And He identifies Himself and the life. In other
words, He gives Himself, the God-life. Only God is eternal.
Yet the life is eternal. Therefore, the life is the God-life.
Thus it is that John writes, "He that hath the Son hath *the*
life. . ." (I John 5:12, ASV). The definite article is there.
It is "the life," the God-life. It is His own actual life that is
bestowed and becomes the property of the believer. Then,
beloved, hear me! Since the Christian is the possessor of the
God-life right now (John 5:24), it is as easy and as rational
to expect God to do that which would condemn Him as it is
for the New Creature, bearing His nature, to do that which
would condemn. Can you conceive of God going to hell?
Neither can I conceive of one bearing His nature and living
His life going to hell.

We come now to the fifth pillar, the

PROTECTION OF GOD

The moment one becomes a Christian, the moment we
commit ourselves to Him, that moment we belong to Him
and become His responsibility. Paul wrote to the Corinthians ". . . ye are Christ's. . ." (I Corinthians 3:23) and
". . . ye are not your own . . . . For ye are bought with a
price. . ." (I Corinthians 6:19, 20). Redemption's price has
been paid by the death of Jesus on the cross. The One who
bought us back is God. We belong to Him.

When this great truth is established, the problem of our
security dissolves into the question, "Is God able to protect
His property?"

Paul said that he could and would. Listen to him! ". . . I
know whom I have believed, and am persuaded that he is

able to keep that which I have committed unto him against
that day" (II Timothy 1:12). Peter says he was "kept by
the power of God through faith." He didn't hold out, God
held him. But someone may ask, "What if you were to lose
your faith?" The answer is, "You can't." Faith is not something arbitrarily bestowed, it is something that is earned.
Christ earned your faith. You became convinced He could
be trusted. That is why you had faith in Him. For that faith
to be destroyed, Christ must do something that would
prove Him untrustworthy. That He will never do.

The author of Hebrews believed God could and would
protect His property, "Wherefore he is able to save them
to the uttermost that come unto God by him. . ." (Hebrews
7:25).

Jude believed it, "Now unto him that is able to keep you
from falling, and to present you faultless before the presence
of his glory. . ." (Jude 24).

And Jesus said emphatically that He could and would.
". . . they shall never perish, neither shall any man pluck
them out of my hand" (John 10:28). The word "man" is
printed in italics to show that it was supplied by the trans-
lators. What Jesus said was nothing, absolutely nothing —
man, demon, or thing — could take a believer out of His
hands. God protects His own.

With joy let us now consider the sixth pillar, the

PRIESTHOOD OF CHRIST

The basic argument of the book of Hebrews is the supe-
riority of Christianity over Judaism. Central in the argument
is the fact that the Christian's high priest is vastly superior
to that of the Jews. The author argues that the Jewish
sacrifice was repeated year after year, yet it was "not possible
that the blood of bulls and of goats should take away sins. . ."
(Hebrews 10:4). Then we read, ". . . every priest standeth
daily ministering and offering oftentimes the same sacrifices,

which can never take away sins: But this man [Christ], after he had offered one sacrifice for sins for ever, sat down on the right hand of God" (Hebrews 10:11, 12). Note it carefully! Neither the tabernacle nor the temple contained seats for the priests. They stood constantly, for their work was never done. But Jesus, after offering Himself, sat down. He alone could say, "It is finished." The perfect sacrifice was offered, and there remaineth no more sacrifice for sin. All that was necessary for atonement was complete. Hence we read, "the blood of Jesus Christ his Son cleanseth us from all sin" (I John 1:7). He didn't say merely past sins, but all sins. He didn't say part of them, but all of them. The author then goes on to say, ". . . we are sanctified through the offering of the body of Jesus Christ once for all" (Hebrews 10:10), and "by one offering he hath perfected for ever them that are sanctified" (verse 14). The perfect sacrifice provides a perfect salvation. That which began in the eternal purpose of God carries us all the way to sanctification and glorification based on that perfect sacrifice.

But our High Priest, after the perfect sacrifice, continues His perfect work. The author of Hebrews furthermore declares, "Wherefore he is able also to save them to the uttermost that come unto God by him, seeing he ever liveth to make intercession for them" (Hebrews 7:25). Paul states, ". . . It is Christ that died, yea rather, that is risen again, who is even at the right hand of God, who also maketh intercession for us" (Romans 8:34). And John records the words, ". . . If any man sin, we have an advocate with the Father, Jesus Christ the righteous" (I John 2:1). If words mean anything, these scriptures declare that we have a living High Priest sitting at the right hand of God and interceding in our behalf. He is One who can be touched with the feeling of our infirmities. When a Christian sins, that High Priest says, "charge that to my account for my blood has already paid for it." An instance of His successful intercession is found in the already mentioned story of Simon Peter (Luke 22:31, 32). Jesus said, "I have prayed for thee." If at any time Simon became a lost soul, then the prayer of that High Priest failed. You have your choice between a safe Simon and a helpless High Priest. But Simon himself declared that he was kept by the power of God. The intercession of Jesus prevailed. It always has as attested by His words, "Those that thou gavest me I have kept, and none of them is lost, but the son of perdition. . . " (John 17:12). That successful High Priest now prays for us. "I pray not that thou shouldest take them out of the world, but that thou shouldest keep them from the evil [one]" (John 17:15). That prayer is always answered.

Jesus was both the sacrifice and the High Priest. He died to save; He lives to keep us saved. Just as the manslayer was safe in the City of Refuge as long as the High Priest lived (Numbers 35:25), so we are safe as long as Jesus lives. Hear His words, ". . . because I live, ye shall live also" (John 14: 19), and He shall never die. Neither shall I.

Briefly let me mention the seventh pillar, the

PERFORMANCE OF THE SPIRIT

The amazing character of salvation is seen in the fact that all three persons of the Trinity are involved in it. The Father loved the world, gave His Son, and purposed man's redemption. On the cross the Son paid redemption's price and rent the veil that barred man from God's presence. But the Spirit is the actual agent of regeneration. It is He that convicts of sin and creates the longing for salvation. It is He that bears witness to Jesus as the Lamb of God atoning for man's sin. And Jesus said, "It is the Spirit that quickeneth. . . " (John 6:63). The same Spirit that brooded over primal matter and produced life; the same Spirit that brooded over Ezekiel's valley of bones and raised a living army; the same Spirit that brooded over the womb of the Virgin Mary that she should bring forth Jesus; that same Spirit broods over a man dead in trespasses and sins, and quickens him into life.

But is His work then through? Has He nothing further to do with the Christian? Listen to Paul! "Being confident of this very thing, that he which hath begun a good work in you will perform it until the day of Jesus Christ" (Philippians 1:6). The same Spirit that performed the miracle of the New Birth will perfect it. All too often He must labor with groanings which cannot be uttered, but He will finish what He started. What He commenced He will consummate. The Bible says so.

And, finally, we come to the eighth pillar, the

PRONOUNCEMENT OF GOD'S WORD

For our last pillar supporting the capstone of the believer's security, we return to our original text. ". . . this is the record, that God hath given to us eternal life, and this life is in his Son" (I John 5:11). That eternal life is not in our being good but in Christ being God. It is in His Son, and "He that hath the Son hath life" (I John 5:12). In John 5:24, Jesus said that the believer should never be brought to trial in a condemnatory proceeding concerning sin much less be condemned. Now note it carefully! The Bible says that God hath given to us eternal life. It is life with neither beginning nor ending. Since God alone innately possesses such life, it is His own quality of life that He bestows. It is God's eternal life that is given. ". . . he that believeth not God hath made him a liar. . . " (I John 5:10).

Brethren, hear me! Until the purposes of God are thwarted and He skulks away in chagrin; until the control of the universe is wrested from His hands; until the creature like a Frankenstein conquers the Creator; until God violates His own nature and becomes a sufferer in hell; until Satan is big enough to defeat the Father, Son, and Holy Spirit; until the sacrifice of Jesus is no better than the death of a dog; until the Spirit goes on a vacation or proves inadequate to finish what He started; until God becomes an unmitigated liar, I am safe.

Amen and Amen! To God be the glory for His positive preservation of those who genuinely trust Him.

*7. Paul Brooks Leath**

THE LOST ARE TO BE EVANGELIZED

Jesus told stories of ordinary and simple things — yet in such a profound way! He spoke of hidden but valuable pearls, of seed-sowing by farmers, of broken fish-nets, of fishermen, of wheat-weed harvesting, of lily-beauty, of grass-frailty, of bird-clothing and numerous other of the common, well-known features of Palestinian life.

And with these stories as framework for hanging great truths, Jesus spoke so convincingly to His contemporaries. His story of the lost coin, lost sheep, and lost son is typical. The mention of the coin, sheep, and son caused no eye-blinking alertness; but when He put "lost" in the account, drama and tenseness were added. At the end, there was rejoicing because each was "found." The incidents of the lost coin and lost sheep seem to be really just introductory to the later part of the story — that of the lost son!

*PAUL BROOKS LEATH received his B.A. degree at Baylor University, his Th.M at Southwestern Baptist Theological Seminary, and his Th. D. at New Orleans Baptist Theological Seminary. After pastoring churches in Louisiana, Georgia, and Texas, he moved to California where he now pastors the Truett Memorial Baptist Church in Long Beach. He was in full time evangelistic work from 1941 to 1947 and carried on other special activities during his ministry.

75

This description of men as "lost" is also found on the lips of Jesus in the Jericho event. Jesus said to Zacchaeus and all those around him that He had come to "seek and to save that which was lost." He had previously charged His disciples to go only to the "lost" sheep of the house of Israel. He mentioned that salt could have its troubles when it "lost" its savor. He told the disciples to pick up fragments of the fish and loaves so that nothing would be "lost." Sad were His words put in question form: "For what is a man profited, if he shall gain the whole world, and lose his own soul? or what shall a man give in exchange for his soul?" (Matthew 16:26). Paul adds to the words of Jesus some of his own: "But if our gospel be hid, it is hid to them that are lost: In whom the god of this world hath blinded the minds of them which believe not, lest the light of the glorious gospel of Christ, who is the image of God, should shine unto them" (II Corinthians 4:3, 4).

Lost! The condition of sinners! The curse of men! The result of sin!

Lost! Lost sons — this drives parents to despair. Lost soldiers — this is an army's plague. Lost fortunes — this prompts suicides. Lost travelers — this calls for action. Lost ways — this calls for guides. Lost health — this fills hospitals. Lost joy and compassion — the Christian's nightmare. Lost remembrance — Israel's tragedy. Lost glory — Ichabod. Lost men — this calls for a Saviour!

Lost! One word in a family of words — all speaking of despair and doom! Ugly, unseemly words . . . fear, worry, anxiety, loneliness, grief, uncertainty, separation, panic, terror, tenseness! And beyond these are others . . . guilt, condemnation, judgment, and doom! Being lost means to be "away from, separated from, apart from, cut-off from." Our word "without" conveys something of the awfulness of the thought.

Man is said to be *Without God.* Paul says it bluntly:

"That at that time ye were without Christ . . . and without God in the world" (Ephesians 2:12). Man's worst plague — to be cut off from people! Among the mentally ill these are known as schizophrenics — not far from mental and social suicide. But, men cut-off and "lost from God" are spiritual suicides.

Without God — this is major. Without health, without family, without wealth, without home, without fortune — these are minor! This is man's only real need in eternity and in this life. The lost man has everything but the one necessity.

Without God's presence. This is Adam and Eve driven from the Garden of Eden. This is Cain — a wanderer: ". . . clouds they are without water, carried about of winds; trees whose fruit withered, without fruit, twice dead, plucked up by the roots; Raging waves of the sea, foaming out their own shame; wandering stars, to whom is reserved the blackness of darkness for ever" (Jude 12, 13).

The five foolish virgins understood what being "without" meant. And so did the man without a wedding garment. In eternity, the sinner shall have finally and eternally that which he has in time now.

Man is said to be *without hope*. Ephesians 2:12 just uses the phrase ". . . having no hope. . . " Sometimes it is difficult to see what being without hope means. We know what losing home, house, family, health, wealth, job, and food means. But losing hope is almost dissociated from these visible things. Being "without hope" needs other words to complete the sentence and to give understanding.

The lost man is without hope of forgiveness of sins. As it was with Cain, so with this man sin always crouches at the door. Life becomes one more massive misery of sins . . . repeated, rapacious, wretched, woeful, wilful, wasteful, hurtful, harassing, hated sins. Man is caught in the squirrel cage of sins. At the same time he runs from some, he runs into and onto others. In dull monotony and stupid drudgery, he stands in a many-sided mirror everywhere facing his sins.

The lost man has no hope of a better tomorrow. Even in the social, earthly, material world, man cannot survive without hope. And without spiritual hope of heaven, life comes to a standstill and stagnation.

Hope is the diamond among the gems, the orchid or rose among the flowers, the sun among the planets, the rainbow in the clouds. Without it to cheer him, he is like the slave driven to the dungeon of despair or the criminal sent to the guillotine of wretchedness.

Man is said to be *without excuse.* This is the conclusion which Paul reaches in the massive and masterful first chapter of Romans. He mentions the "wrath of God" in verse eighteen. He speaks of being "without excuse" in verse twenty. He sums up as "worthy of death" in verse thirty-two. Someone reminds us that we all have at least three things: complaints, pains, and excuses! In heaven, we will have none of the first two and will not need the last. In hell, the sinner will have an abundance of complaints and pains but excuses won't be recognized. It is interesting to note that to most of us, failures, problems and the like don't cause us so much anxiety — if we have excuses for them. The sinner has plenty of excuses now, but he won't have any in eternity.

Man is without excuse for his sin. Without excuse for being ignorant of God. Without excuse for being lost. Without excuse for rejecting Christ. Without excuse for unpreparedness. Without excuse for being condemned.

No excuse admitted the five foolish virgins through the shut door. The laborer in the vineyard had no excuse when his lord asked for an accounting. The prodigal never gave an excuse for his vagrancy. Zacchaeus made no excuse for his sins in Jericho. The repentant thief offered no excuse for his life at the cross. Adam and Eve fabricated excuses, but they were not recognized. Abraham excused himself but God did not. Moses attempted excuse, but was foiled. Judas tried it and died!

Now to this awful condition of the world, *We Are Witnesses!* The world needs not statisticians, not analysts, not prescriptions, not advice, but *witnesses*, messengers, apostles, prophets! This is what Jesus sent the Seventy and the Twelve to do. This is what we are to do as we go into all the world. Jesus said: " . . . and ye shall be witnesses unto me both in Jerusalem, and in all Judaea, and in Samaria, and unto the uttermost part of the earth" (Acts 1:8).

This was what Naaman needed, and it is what the Hebrew maid gave. Joshua and Caleb brought back a good witness from their viewing of Canaan, and God rewarded them. The Twelve and the Seventy went forth as heralds of Christ, and miracles followed them. At the witnessing of the apostles at Pentecost, salvation came to multitudes. Resulting from the witnessing of the woman at the well Sychar's citizens were changed. Following the witnessing of Philip in Samaria, the city was converted. At the preaching of Jonah, Nineveh was spared!

What was the plan Jesus suggested for His followers? It is found plainly outlined in the tenth chapter of Luke; and once again the word "without" comes into prominence.

Witnessing was to be done *without regard for audience.* They were to go into specified cities and preach to any or to all who would listen. Isaiah had none to hear and heed his message; Billy Graham has had tens of thousands. John the Baptist had Jerusalem's and Judaea's multitudes, but Stephen was stoned as a benediction to his first and only sermon. Wesley had his crowds but Bunyan had prison inmates. The Seventy were to go as lambs among wolves. What valor! Could this be ours today?

Witnessing was to be done *without regard for their person.* Jesus had earlier reminded His followers that they were to

"hate" father, mother, brother, sister . . . even their own lives.
There are some things that we can leave to God, and this is
one of them! What happens to the Christian worker is rel-
atively unimportant. It is the witnessing that is crucial. A
young Communist worker replied to questioners about his
loyalty to his work. I paraphrase his answer as follows: "I
am a Communist, and I am proud of it. My work is to take
the truths I embrace to all who will listen to me as well as
to those who will not. My work is my life and my breath,
my meat and my drink. My loyalty to Communist ideals is
greater than my love for pleasure, for clothing, and for possessions. What happens to me is unimportant; what happens
to Communist ideals is everything."

Witnessing was to be done *without regard for remunera-
tion.* Taking no scrip nor purse could mean that the disciples
were not to go on a shopping expedition. It could also mean
that they were to depend utterly upon God and on those
who heard them! One has to live, to eat, and to clothe himself — to be sure. One must show concern for earthly things.
But deep down in everyone of us is the burning desire to be
cast out on nothing but the grace and mercy of God to see
what would happen. This is what the Reformers did. Early
evangelists in America did this. Judson, Carey, Rice, and
others did this. The only thing the Seventy and the Twelve
had was a witness to give . . . and this was enough!

I remember hearing Dr. Charles Culpepper, Sr., saying
that when the Communists came to his home and stripped
him of all earthly goods and friends, he then had nothing on
earth left except his Christian faith. In this state of affairs,
he said, "I never felt so great in all my life."

Witnessing was to be done *without regard for results.* This
does not mean to be disinterested in results, but it means to
leave the results to God. Jesus warned them that some
would hear and heed the message while others would reject.
He even turned and pronounced judgment upon Bethsaida,

Chorazin, and Capernaum. Isaiah was sent to preach and witness to his generation, but the response was to be nil. But, God saw to it that a witness was made!

C. T. Studd embodied these truths in his life. The famous, wealthy, and gifted sportsman of England heard and read poignant words of a missionary, then gave up a legal career, gave away his fortune of one-half million dollars, and spent his life in Africa as a missionary — the last thirteen years being without a furlough.

Mrs. Lucille Wilson, Ralph Zook, and Stamy Edmisten of Alamosa, Colorado, cooperated to save the lives of thirteen men on a C-46 military transport when the airship was in trouble and attempted to land in a blinding snow storm. As the plane buzzed the town, alert citizens began a series of telephone calls which in time sent Edmisten, an airline employee, to the airport to quickly light the landing field. Ralph Zook, the railroad dispatcher started it all when he first heard the disabled aircraft. The telephone operator continued it until she found the employee of the airlines. It all began with those chilling words from the dispatcher, "Listen! There it buzzes again! It's lost!"

Through so simple a thing as continuous witnessing, world conversion could be possible in 32 days! If all were faithful to pass on the gospel story one to another, all the world could hear the Gospel in 32 days. If only one witnessed to another on the first day of the month, then those two to two other, those four to four other and so on consecutively through 32 days, then by that time 2,148,139,008 people would have heard the story of Jesus.

Paul would tell us to be witnesses in season and out of season, in the church and out of the church, in character and by word of mouth, in life and in death. David Brainerd, missionary to the American Indians, said, "I care not how or where I live, or what hardships I go through, so that I can but gain souls for Christ." Matthew Henry wrote, "I would think it a greater happiness to gain one soul to Christ than mountains of silver and gold to myself." Fletcher of Madeley said to Samuel Bradburn, "If you should live to preach the Gospel 40 years and be the instrument of saving only one soul it would be worth all your labors."

Make the call, tell the story, give of yourself! For men are lost . . . and we are witnesses!

8. *William M. Jones**

THE PERSONS INVOLVED IN EVANGELISM

"And he brought him to Jesus. . ." (John 1:42).

"What do you consider to be the greatest challenge facing teenagers today?" This question was asked in a survey of young people in Catholic high schools from widely separated communities as Seattle and Miami. They listed as their number one challenge, "Bringing others to faith in Christ."

The true Christian is not one who simply belongs to an ethical system called Christianity, but one regenerated by the power of the Holy Spirit, walking in the Spirit, living triumphantly daily in the living Christ, whom he loves, serves and shares. We have failed to share redemption and have become "cliquish" and "clannish" and are "witnesses unto ourselves" instead of "unto Him."

Our big task today is to get the "church out of the church."

* WILLIAM M. JONES is a graduate of Lenoir-Rhyne College, Hickory, North Carolina and Southwestern Baptist Seminary, Forth Worth, Texas. He has served pastorates in Florida, South Carolina, North Dakota and North Carolina. He is currently pastor of the First Baptist Church in Clinton, North Carolina.

The true purpose of every worship service is to get the Christian ready to witness. Worship continues to be a form instead of a force — a form of escapism. Too many are seeking "sanctuary." We have produced congregations composed largely of dilettantes, who follow Christ superficially or as a pastime.

The early Christians had a good sun tan. They spent most of their time out of doors witnessing, for this was their life. They went from house to house and many of them lost their lives and were scattered abroad. It is not easy to be a witness for Christ. The very word "witness" in the Greek is the word "martureo," from which we get our word martyr. It is an expensive thing to be a soul winner. Legally, a witness is one who testifies for some one who is on trial. Christ is on trial today in every business, school, store, and in every city and community. Our task is to witness for Him.

To bring men to Jesus there are three essentials.

THE SAVIOUR

". . . We have found the Messias, which is being interpreted, the Christ" (John 1:41). What we think of Christ will determine what we think of the Atonement, Resurrection, Second Coming, and the Great Commission. The reason man needs a Saviour is that man is a sinner by birth, by nature, and by choice. As a sinner his initial need is a Saviour, not an example, pattern, or guide. We must believe not only what God said about His Son as Saviour and Lord, but in order to be saved we must also believe what God says about man as a sinner. We must agree with God concerning His Son and we must agree with God concerning us as sons of men. The hardest part about admitting that we are sinners, is admitting that all of our good, apart from the righteousness of Christ, is also evil in God's sight. Man readily condemns the baser sins, but how rarely do we see one condemning all his good as evil, and all his works apart from Christ as dead works, and utterly worthless in God's sight?

One day, while walking down the streets of San Francisco, I saw a man rolling himself along on a wagon made of skate wheels. The man had no legs, and was strapped to the wagon but was able to make rapid progress by pushing himself along with his hands. We came to the intersection about the same time. He rolled out to the street car track and came perilously close to the tracks and stopped. I wondered how he would get aboard the street car, and waited to see. The car rolled up, stopped and the doors opened. The man on the wagon smiled and threw his hands above his head. A kindly conductor smiled, reached down and lifted him in. There I staggered in my sins on the street and cried out to God, "There I am Lord, I don't have a leg to stand on." I, at last, threw my arms up to God as a helpless sinner, not trying to stand on my education, ordination, or commission, or anything else in this world. The Great Conductor of the universe lifted me in.

Just a few days before his execution as a British spy, during the Revolutionary War, Major Andre wrote these lines:

> Hail Sovereign love which first began
> That scheme to rescue fallen man,
> Hail that matchless, free eternal grace
> Which gave my soul a hiding place.
>
> Against the God who built the sky
> I fought with hands uplifted high,
> Despised the mentioning of his grace
> Too proud to seek a hiding place.
>
> Enwrapted in thick Egyptian night,
> Fond of darkness more than light,
> Madly, I ran the sinful race
> Secure without a hiding place.

But thus the eternal counsels ran
Almighty love, arrest that man,
I felt the arrows of distress
As they pierced my sinful breast.

To Sinai's fiery mount I fled
For refuge I vainly pled,
But justice cried with frowning face
This mount is no hiding place.

On Jesus, God's vengeance fell
That would have sent a world to Hell,
But He bore it all for a sinful race
And thus became their hiding place.

Should seven fold of thunder roll
And shake this globe from pole to pole,
It shall not daunt my face
For in Jesus, I've found a hiding place.

Just a few more setting suns at most
Shall land my soul on Canaan's fair coast,
Where I shall forever sing the songs of grace
And tell of my glorious hiding place.

THE SOUL WINNER

What did you do today that only a Christian could do? There can only be one answer — "I witnessed to an unsaved person concerning Jesus." You will never be unique as a Christian until you win someone to Jesus. Everything that you do as a Christian can be duplicated by the unsaved. You say, "I gave money to the church" — unsaved people give to the church. You say, "I try to live right" — the unsaved can say the same thing. You say, "I believe in living by the Golden Rule" — the unsaved can say the same. But when you engage in the business of "witnessing" for Jesus, you are doing something that no unsaved person can do.

If your neighbor was dying and knowing that you were a Christian, and sent for you to tell him how to become a

Christian, could you lead him to Jesus and give him the assurance of his salvation? This is the supreme test. Let's not confuse witnessing with invitations to attend church, Sunday school, or any other church function. The task of the soul winner is to bring the individual to Jesus! Salvation is of God and God alone. God never *told* Noah to go into the Ark. He *invited* Noah to come into the Ark. Almighty God was the first to enter the Ark, and the last to leave. Our task is to invite, remembering the invitation is from Jesus, and we are to extend it as attractively and winsomely as we can.

Let me suggest four simple facts that will enable you to be more effective as a soul winner. A soul winner —

Learns. Jesus said, ". . . learn of me. . ." (Matthew 11: 29). Volumes have been written about soul winning, but there's only one way to be a soul winner — simply find a prospect and *"share"* with him what Jesus has done for you. When God saved me, I knew only one verse in the Bible, John 3:16, but that one verse was enough to lead my father to Jesus.

Alexander Pope said, "A little learning is a dangerous thing." This wouldn't be true if we realize whatever we know is but a little. If you furnish the Lord with a surrendered life, He will give you the ability to do anything He asks — "Learn of me." Greek, Hebrew and Latin have their place, but their place is not where Pilate put them, over the head of Jesus, but rather at His feet. I heard of a woman, who having just found the Lord, was asked to give her testimony. Her speech was poor and she was limited in formal training, but she gave a glowing testimony. When she finished, one was heard to say, "She's a nut." The new convert, hearing the remark, turned and smiling said, "I may be a nut, but I'm screwed to a mighty good bolt." Lenin said, "I'd rather have ten fools than ten thousand placid followers."

Everyone is someone's fool — whose are you? I'd rather be a fool for Jesus, than anyone I know.

Labors. It takes work to bring a soul to Jesus in keeping with the character of Christ. Zion must travail to bring into being physical children and so must we travail to bring spiritual children into God's Kingdom. One can call on prospects, hand out cards, issue an invitation, but to sit down with the Bible and explain just what a Christian is and how one becomes a child of God, and then keep going back until you have won that person — that takes a labor of love. With all due respect to our planning and programming, and even our preaching and our praying, I believe our need now is an "All out, every day, door to door" effort to bring men to Jesus. God never commanded a sinner to go to church, but He does command the church to go to the people.

A Sunday school teacher told his class of Junior boys to bring an object the following Sunday, that would illustrate a verse of Scripture. Next Sunday they came with their objects. The first boy brought a salt shaker and said, "Jesus said, 'Ye are the salt of the earth.' " The second boy brought a candle and said, "Ye are the light of the world." The third brought a Bantam egg. The teacher was puzzled and asked, "Is that an egg?" The boy replied, "Yes, it's a Bantam egg." The teacher asked, "And what Scripture does that illustrate?" The boy said, "She hath done what she could."

Lives. Jesus represents us in heaven and we represent Him on earth. What kind of representatives are we? Paul said, "For to me to live is Christ. . . " (Philippians 1:21). Not *as* Christ, not *like* Christ, But *"is"* Christ. I heard one say of another, "He says such great things! Isn't it a pity he has no right to say them?" G. Campbell Morgan said he was asked to recommend a young pastor for a church in England. The committee said "we want a pastor who is a good mixer." Dr. Morgan replied by saying, "The only place for a good mixer is in the kitchen. A man cannot be a jackass six days a week and a prophet of the Lord on the seventh."

Loves. Jesus asked Peter, " . . . lovest thou me?" (John 21: 16). Not do you love sheep, tending sheep, but do you love *Me!* We have heard much about a passion for souls. What we need is not a passion for souls but rather a passion for Jesus. For when we love Him we will love souls and do our best to bring them to Him. I remember knocking on the door of a home where I could see all the way to the back. Everything about the place was repulsive; the yard, porch, living room and kitchen. Unkept and unclean. I wondered if my people would welcome them into the church. I knocked twice and started to leave, feeling that I had done my duty. As I went down the steps, a voice spoke to me, "If I can love these people, so can you." I stopped and said, "Yes, Lord, and I know You love them." I went to the back of the house, found a family of ten picking peas, joined in the picking with them and later won all ten to Jesus, and they became some of our most loyal and dedicated members.

The Sinner

He is there across the world, across the street, down the street, at home, everywhere. Waiting for you to come and share your Jesus with them.

Several years ago while conducting a revival in Jacksonville, Florida, I was standing outside a hotel waiting for the pastor. It was pouring rain and two Negro bell hops were talking, and one said, "Look out there at that rain. Don't you hate days like this?" His friend answered, words I'll never forget, "Naw! I don't hate this day, I ain't ever had it before and I'm shore glad I'se got it and I'm going out there and git all of it I can!"

When I saw the rain, I too felt like the first bell hop, until the other spoke and what he said changed my entire day. I said, "Lord, I've never had this day before. I hope You'll give me all of it. Now help me to use it for You. Lead me to some soul and give me just the words I need to bring that soul to you."

" . . . he that winneth souls is wise" (Proverbs 11:30). If you want to live when this old world is burned to a cinder and the stars fall from their orbits like sparks from a blacksmith's anvil, then make soul-winning your main task, and like Daniel, your testimony will please God.

A pastor, who had been ill for a long time, knowing that the end was not far off, told his wife, "If you ever decide that I need such a useless thing as a grave stone, please have these words inscribed on the stone: 'And [they] heard him speak, and they followed Jesus' (John 1:37)." God grant, each time we speak, our hearers will want to follow Jesus.

While President of Asbury College in Wilmore, Kentucky, Dr. H. C. Morrison was given a trip around the world for a preaching mission. He was away six months, preaching throughout the world to the Chinese, Japanese, Indians, Arabs, and Africans. He sailed for home on the same ship that was carrying Teddy Roosevelt, back from a safari in Africa. The passengers aboard were anxious to see the President, and every newspaper from the States carried stories of his exploits in Africa. Finally they landed in New York and multitudes gathered to welcome Roosevelt back home. Bands played, confetti flew and the sidewalks were jammed with people to see Roosevelt.

Dr. Morrison said, "We had to wait until the President and his party disembarked, and while waiting I scanned the shore to see if anyone had come to welcome me. I didn't see *one* familiar face — no one had come to welcome me home. I learned later an epidemic had caused the college to be quarantined. I was so disappointed I left and went below to my room. Feeling so let down, I fell on my knees and cried, 'Lord, I've been around this world telling men about You and how much You love them. I've looked into black faces, yellow faces, red faces, and tried to tell them about you. I haven't been shooting lions, buffalo, and rhinos. Yet, look at that crowd that welcomes him home! Lord, not a single person came to welcome me home.'"

Dr. Morrison said, "I felt an unseen presence standing at my side, and touching me on the shoulder said, 'Preacher, you're not home yet . . . you're not home yet.'"

9. *Emory L. Williams**

THE POWER FOR EVANGELISM

"For John truly baptized with water; but ye shall be baptized with the Holy Ghost not many days hence" (Acts 1:5).

THE HOLY SPIRIT IN A REVIVAL

The waning power of the church is a favorite topic in many circles today. Many who make up the church today are minus this victory-giving power. The angels weep when they see the average Christian today. We stand in the midst of a world sick nigh unto death. Other doctors have failed. The trouble with so much of our Christian work today is that it is not divinely planned and divinely wrought.

One great religious organization speaks in the name of Christianity and calls upon men everywhere to enter the

---

*EMORY L. WILLIAMS is a graduate of Emory University, Candler Theological Seminary, the University of Tennessee, and he pursued special studies at Southern Baptist Theological Seminary in Louisville, Kentucky. Jefferson City, Tennessee. Having pastored large churches in Georgia and Tennessee, he has studied under a scholarship in Psychology and Psychiatry at the University of Tennessee. He has also taught in several schools, served on the executive board of the state of Tennessee, and on other committees and boards.

fold of an infallible church. It tells those who are outside
of its portals that salvation is found only in the bosom of its
organization. This church stands mighty, colossal, and impressive with its complex organization and extravagant
claims, and replete with mystery for the simple minded.
She demands blind obedience and unquestioned loyalty.

On the other hand are the host of people who call themselves Protestants. They deny the infallible church with its
absolute head and insist upon the right of the private interpretation of the Word of God, but among them are found
various degrees of ritualism and confusion of beliefs. There
are those who ignore denominational lines such as mod-
ernists, fundamentalists, liberals and conservatives. There
are vast voices claiming to speak for each of them. Some of
them emphasize the deity of Christ, His virgin birth, His
atoning death, His bodily resurrection, the new birth, the
work of the Holy Spirit and the personal return of our Lord.
Many of them hold all of these doctrines. Others accept
them with different degrees of emphasis. Extreme mod-
ernists no longer claim any sure word of prophecy. They
are, in fact, not sure of anything.

Here in our text is a promise, bright like the light when
the morning dawneth and that graces the dew when the
eventide cometh. It is like a star of hope shining through
a rift in the black thunderstorm clouds of a long night. It is
like a warm spring morning after a long, hard winter with its
warm radiant sun enveloping the earth. It is a voice of hope
out of an age of despair. It is a vibrant note, sweet as a
song, as musical as a heavenly orchestra. "But ye shall be
baptized with the Holy Ghost not many days hence."

If we would be heartened and encouraged concerning a
great revival of spiritual power today we need to turn back
and read and study conditions, preceding, during and following Pentecost. Pentecost is made more meaningful because

of the background against which it stands. No background is so black, no day so spiritually hopeless, no night so long in despair, no condition so discouraging but that the irresistible power of God can cope with it.

Today there is hope and keen expectancy on the part of many concerning a revival. Such hope and expectancy are not an empty dream, but are well-founded with substantial support by God's Word and by the march of Christianity through the ages. Tides of spiritual power seem to swing from one extreme to another. Today we feel the need, the indispensableness of a revival. The outlook is not hopeless; it is hopeful. If God could give a Pentecost two thousand years ago, can He give one now? He is the same yesterday, today and forever. If He could convert Nineveh in a day's time, if He can turn a nation to Him on Carmel heights in one day, He can turn America and the world to Himself now. If Christianity had the power to subdue the wicked in the Roman Empire nineteen hundred years ago in spite of Rome's relentless persecution, Christianity has power to subdue the wicked empires today.

Not only are God's children promised the Holy Spirit they are warned positively that God's work can be done in no other way. ". . . Not by might, nor by power, but by my Spirit, saith the Lord of hosts" (Zechariah 4:6). For the Kingdom of God is not in word but in power. The people in our world are bewildered and confused. There is need of a message of hope and assurance. In the aching heart of humanity there is a void that the world can never fill. In man's desperate need, in his helpless condition and his dire extremity, conscious of his irreparable loss, he turns to God and wails in his pitiful and penitent cry for help. People are sick, hungry-hearted and needy — and their need is to turn to God. America needs a great revival! It will be a Holy Spirit revival or chaos in America. Which will it be?

Today the bleak winds of destiny are howling in protest to the way we are living, but the dark, benighted days in which we live with their noisy contrary winds and terrible sounds may be but the herald of the dawn of a mighty, sweeping spiritual awakening. Does your heart not respond? O God, may it be so!

THE SOUL WINNER SHOULD UNDERSTAND THE OFFICE WORK OF THE HOLY SPIRIT

"Even the Spirit of truth; whom the world cannot receive, because it seeth him not, neither knoweth him: but ye know him; for he dwelleth with you, and shall be in you" (John 14: 17).

Study to know Him, that He is a person and not just an object. Say "He" and not "it." Know that He is God, know His will, know His voice, know His calling. We are to try the spirits. "Beloved, believe not every spirit, but try the spirits whether they are of God. . . " (I John 4:1). We must understand that the Holy Spirit never leads you to do a sinful, mean, little or selfish thing. The Holy Spirit never leads you contrary to the Word of God. We can know Greek and Hebrew and church organization. We can organize to the nth degree but until we know Him in all of His fullness and come to yield ourselves as instruments in the hands of the Holy Spirit we can not know His call when He speaks to the individual saved by the grace of God.

It is true that we are many rather than mighty. This has left us powerless. There is no question about our number. More people belong to Christian churches than ever before. So-called Christian nations are the greatest in the world. The great ones of the earth are numbered among Christian people. The rulers of nations, the kings of finance are in our churches. Men and women who have created literature, who are leaders in science and masters in every form of art have their names on our rolls. The money of the world is large in the coffers of people who call themselves Christians. All the world must testify to the unselfish service of the people called Christians.

Yet we are forced to confess the power that came at Pentecost is not being manifest. The real work of the church is to bring sinners to repentance and produce saints who are mighty witnesses of righteousness. Jesus promised that the Holy Spirit should give power for the fulfillment of the Great Commission. Those Christians were neither numerous nor wealthy; they lacked social prestige; they were wanting in the training from the schools but they had power. The Jerusalem church did not own a place of meeting and its greatest preacher had no money when confronted with an object of charity, but it was strong enough to rise victorious above stoning, prison and the sword.

Today with our culture and prestige of wealth we are weak and hesitating. By all the standards men have for greatness we ought to be one thousand times stronger than that early church but we are not. The number of lost people in our land is appalling. The power remains but our self-indulgence, our love of ease will not let us pay the price which its possession demands. We count big on the muster-rolls of our churches but not so much on the battle-line of the kingdom. We are broad in the scope of our enterprise but lacking in the intensity that means power. We have lost much of the spirit of sacrifice and have forgotten how to pray without ceasing. Revivals come about because men pray. Prayer is opening the door to let God in and do for us what we cannot do for ourselves.

Spiritual power! When the church of Jesus Christ and God's men are on their knees the kingdom of God will advance and the lost will come to know Christ, the Saviour and Lord; but until we are filled with the Holy Spirit of Christ we can not make an impression upon a distorted world.

WE ARE DEPENDENT UPON THE HOLY SPIRIT
TO CONVICT THE WORLD OF SIN

Crumbling convictions have contributed to our weakness. Convictions are mighty things. We do not hold them; they hold us. We hold opinions; we are held by convictions. Convictions do not matter about some things, but things like life and death, time and eternity, salvation and doom must be deep and abiding. It is convicted men and women who plough deep furrows in the field of time. Men who have convictions about liberty, defy tyrants, and lead revolutions. Convictions concerning their religion made crusaders and martyrs.

Those who find nothing in their religion to hold and challenge their deepest nature will drift with the tides to rest and die upon barren shores. We have not forgotten our articles of faith. We would still defend them vigorously but they do not grip and master us. We view with a sort of pathetic complacency the gradual crumbling of their majestic structure. We have acquired a sort of slip-shod mental attitude toward their value. It no longer shocks us that a preacher denies the deity of our Lord, His bodily resurrection or His personal return. He says a few words about brotherly love and pearly human virtue. We are not troubled much when one of our number ridicules the blood of the cross if he is sweet-spirited and so phrases his teaching as to offend no one.

Beware of the man who can stand cold-bloodedly and watch the destruction of sacred things. Convictions bring power. Convictions are not always comfortable nor do they make life easy. It was an over-mastering conviction that sent Paul with his scarred body, weary and persecuted, over the world. It was a persuasion that some things are worth dying for that sent Huss to the stake and made others martyrs. Bunyan could have escaped lonely years in that old jail by being less convicted of his faith but the world would have been poorer if it had not been for his convictions.

The conviction that men without Christ are lost has been weakened in our churches and we are not moved to the earnestness that warned with tears. The man or woman with such conviction is not in harmony with our lukewarm, easy-going age. We need fires lightened by the Holy Ghost that our souls may be melted and our convictions of truth remolded and crystallized. God give us convictions!

" . . . You hath he quickened, who were dead in trespasses and sins" (Ephesians 2:1). The Holy Spirit alone can awaken and quicken the unsaved. Preachers, Bible teachers, theologians have tried to do it but have woefully failed.

Futility has marked the effort of all who have tried to awaken the unsaved with their own power. " . . . when he is come, he will reprove the world of sin, and of righteousness, and of judgment" (John 16:8). On the day of Pentecost when the Spirit had come, conviction came also.

The Holy Spirit Is Indispensable in Conversion

The most devout and most eloquent preacher in the world cannot convert one soul. This is the work of the Holy Spirit. Jesus said, "Verily, verily I say unto thee, Except a man be born of water and of the Spirit, he cannot enter into the kingdom of God" (John 3:5). God by His Spirit makes all things new. To make things new is the work of the Holy Spirit. To make things new is the work of God. To make things new is the work of the heart. The Spirit of God working in His children changes them from retreating powers into an army of conquering, militant soldiers of the cross.

No humanistic philosophy of life can change the heart of man and make him partaker of the nature of God except the Holy Spirit. He is God's overseer; He is God's executive in the world; He is the only one who can bring a soul out of darkness into light. This regeneration is of divine origin.

John 1:13, "Which were born, not of blood, nor of the will of the flesh, nor of the will of man, but of God." Joining the church, reformation, good resolutions, education, culture is not the new birth. The new birth is of divine origin. It comes from God into the life of the sinner who believes in Christ. The Holy Spirit leads him to believe and to accept Christ as Saviour and Lord.

In II Corinthians 5:17 we read, "Therefore if any man be in Christ, he is a new creature: old things are passed away; behold, all things are become new." By their fruit you shall know them, and too many with their name on our church rolls seemingly do not have the fruit of a regenerated soul. As we read the Bible it clearly teaches us the fruit of a Christian.

The revival needed is one to revive those who have been saved and bring regeneration to those who do not know Christ as Saviour and make new creatures in Christ Jesus out of them. We are powerless to save men and women. We can not win them to faith in Christ without the agency and help of the Holy Spirit in this dark hour.

10. *W. A. Criswell* *

THE COMMAND TO BE FILLED
WITH THE HOLY SPIRIT

"And be not drunk with wine, wherein is excess; but be filled with the Spirit" (Ephesians 5:18).

The Greek words used in this pointed command are *plerousthe en pneumati,* "to be filled with the Spirit." Aside from the fact that through inspired writers God employed the Greek language to create His New Testament, the words in the original language are most interesting and meaningful in themselves. Let us look at the mandate closely.

*DR. W. A. CRISWELL is one of the most articulate spokesmen of the Christian church today. His wise insight into the vast concepts of Christianity have placed him in the forefront of Christian leadership.

Coupled with his articulate skill is his remarkable facility as a Bible expositor. His studies in the various books of the Bible have won acclaim from every shade in the theological spectrum. He is widely respected and listened to, wherever the Word of God is honored.

Dr. W. A. Criswell is one of the "leading lights" in the Southern Baptist Convention. In fact, the church he pastors, the First Baptist Church of Dallas, Texas, is one of the largest in the world, with more than 15,000 members and an annual budget of more than one and one-half million dollars. The auditorium of the First Baptist Church seats nearly 4,000 and Dr. Criswell faces a crowded auditorium at nearly every service.

God Commands That We Be Filled With the Spirit

Notice that the word *plerousthe* is in the imperative mood. It is a mandate. There is never a command that we be baptized by the Spirit, or that we be sealed or indwelt by the Spirit. These are positional; they refer to something God does for us, as writing our names in the Book of Life. The command that we be filled with the Spirit relates not to our position before God but to our daily service and walk. For, you see, a believer can be a carnal, worldly, unfruitful Christian. The New Testament looks upon a man as a trichotomy. He is made up of three parts. There is the *somatikos* man, the body man (from *soma*, "body") (I Timothy 4: 8). There is the *psukikos* man, the sensuous, volital man (from *psuche*, the self as the seat of the affections and will) (I Corinthians 2:14). There is the *pneumatikos* man, the spiritual man (from *pneuma*, "breath," "spirit") (I Corinthians 2:15). But the Christian believer, this *pneumatikos* man, can be also a *sarkikos* man, a fleshly, carnal man (from *sarx*, "flesh") (I Corinthians 3:4). The carnal man lives by the power and dictates of the flesh. The truly spiritual man lives by the power and dictates of the Spirit of God (Galatians 5:16, 17).

The Filling a Repeated Experience

Notice that the verb *plerousthe* is in the present tense. "Tense" to us in the English language means "time." We cannot say anything in English without placing it in some "tense," in some time, as past, present, future. But what we call "tense" in Greek verbs is not "tense" at all. Greek verbs express kinds of action, as a point (aorist), continuous as going on (present), having been completed and remaining completed (perfect), etc. This verb *plerousthe*, therefore, being in what is called the present tense, refers to enduring, continuous action. The translation literally would be, "Be ye being continuously filled with the Holy Spirit."

The experience is repeated again and again. A Christian living a normal life of moment by moment yieldingness to God experiences a moment fullness of the Spirit. Some men experience a spectacular, miraculous, unique fullness that stands out over all other fillings like a mountain peak in a lofty range, like the lone grandeur of a Kilimanjaro in Africa or a Fujiyama in Japan. Such men of marvelous witness and testimony are John Wesley, Charles G. Finney, Dwight L. Moody, and R. A. Torrey. They had one great filling of the Spirit that stood out above all others. (Some of them, as R. A. Torrey, improperly call it "the baptism of the Holy Spirit.") But most of us experience the filling of the Spirit in repeated succession like a mountain chain or many equal peaks. Each day's work brings its measure of endowment and inspiration.

Notice that the verb *plerousthe* is plural in number. The command is addressed not only to the pastor, the preacher, the deacon, the Sunday school teacher, but to every Christian and to every church member. The Ephesian letter from which this text is taken is a circular letter. When Paul wrote it, he most likely left the salutation blank, so that the name of the church could be later inserted. In some ancient manuscripts the word "Ephesus" is omitted. In other ancient manuscripts the name "Laodicea" is written in, most certainly in keeping with the Laodicean letter referred to in Colossians 4:16. All of this gives emphasis to the fact that the injunction that we be filled with Spirit is addressed to all churches, all leaders, all Christians everywhere through all times and generations.

The Man Under the Influence of the Spirit

Notice, lastly, that the verb *plerousthe* is in the passive voice. The subject is acted upon (as in English grammar, the passive voice is illustrated in the sentence, "He is carried," "He is swept away"). It is we who are acted upon by the Holy Spirit. In the complete text, "And be not drunk with wine, wherein is excess; but be filled with the Spirit," Paul is using an illustration of a man who is acted upon, dominated, controlled by something other than himself. The comparison is between the man under the influence of alcohol and the man under the influence of the Holy Spirit. Paul describes the man under the domination of alcohol as "asotia," translated "excess" but a word which really refers to a "course of abandonment" (cf. Titus 1:6; I Peter 1:4).

When the man is drunk with wine and is given over to the influence of liquor, he is a changed person. Sometimes a most neatly groomed and dressed individual becomes disheveled, untidy, and downright dirty. Sometimes a shy, reticent man now talks loud and laughs uproariously. Sometimes a fellow who would never sing in his life now sings at the top of his voice. Sometimes a poor creature so inhibited that he is afraid of his own shadow now becomes as bold as a lion with courage to attempt anything.

I heard of two inebriates, one of whom leaped out the window to fly around the block. In the hospital, when the other one came to see him, the much bandaged and broken-up patient said to his friend, "Why did you let me do it?" His friend replied, "I thought you could!" Under the domination of the Holy Spirit, we also are changed persons. We are doing what we never thought of doing. We are saying what we never thought of saying. We are attempting what we never thought of attempting. In God we are different, changed people.

At Pentecost the ascended Saviour poured out the Holy Spirit upon the world without measure (John 3:34). He is here in all His heavenly presence and miracle-working power. Having come, the Spirit jealously desires the whole of us. James, the Lord's brother and the pastor of the Church at Jerusalem, wrote a tremendously strong statement in James 4:5 — ". . . The spirit that dwelleth in us lusteth to envy." The Greek verb translated "lusteth" is *epipotheo* which means "to desire earnestly," "to long for." In 1611, when the King James version of the Scriptures was made, the word "lusteth" was an exact translation of *epipotheo.* But "lust" to us today has come to have another and unspiritual meaning. James meant that the Holy Spirit so desires to possess us that He envied other loves and interests that command our affection. Think of it! The Holy Spirit of God envying anything that we love more than Him! The verse is enough to make us weep for contrition in our very souls.

For the Spirit to have us, we must yield ourselves to Him. We must be emptied of self to be filled with all of His fullness. Our hands cannot be filled with other things if they are to know the fullness of God. Our hearts cannot be filled with wordly affection and ambition if we are to possess the Spirit without measure. Our souls must be emptied of self when we bring them to the fountains of heaven for the blessing. It seems that Paul's motto was "not I, but Christ. . ." (Galatians 2:20). Oh, that we could surrender ourselves to a like commitment! As we grow in grace, maybe at first it was all of self and none of Thee. Then, it was some of self and some of Thee. Then it was less of self and more of Thee. But now, God grant it, it is none of self and all of Thee. "Filled with the Spirit."